Ditto with the Workshop Book.
Palm Springs 2009.

ELIZABETH ZIMMERMANN'S
KNITTING WORKSHOP

Books by Elizabeth Zimmermann

KNITTING WITHOUT TEARS

KNITTER'S ALMANAC

KNITTING WORKSHOP

Elizabeth Zimmermann's

KNITTING
WORKSHOP

Written and Illustrated

by

ELIZABETH ZIMMERMANN

Photographs

by

MEG SWANSEN

SCHOOLHOUSE PRESS

First printing, 1981
Second printing, 1982
Third printing, 1983
Fourth printing, 1984
Fifth printing, 1985
Sixth printing, 1986
Seventh printing, 1988
Eighth printing, 1991
Ninth printing, 1993
Tenth printing, 1996

ISBN 0-942018-00-1

Schoolhouse Press
6899 Cary Bluff
Pittsville, WI 54466

Library of Congress Cataloging-in-Publication Data

Zimmermann, Elizabeth
    Knitting Workshop: handknitting from Beginnings
    to Master Classes. Accompanying the video series of
    the same name.   81-52967

ACKNOWLEDGEMENTS :

To the Gaffer, and his magnificent
display of Patience & Fortitude during
the gestation of this book.

Also to our dear kids, Chris and
Meg Swansen who did <u>all</u> the work
(I had all the enjoyment) and who
cossetted me.

Television series by Elizabeth Zimmermann:

THE BUSY KNITTER - PBS

THE BUSY KNITTER II - PBS

ELIZABETH ZIMMERMANN'S
KNITTING WORKSHOP - Schoolhouse Press

Editor's Preface:

In the spring of 1981, we approached
Elizabeth about recording the knowledge
she presents during her annual week-
long Knitting Camp.

The resulting video series, ELIZABETH
ZIMMERMANN'S KNITTING WORKSHOP, is
available on VHS from Schoolhouse Press and
shows the Master Knitter & Instructor from an
intimate viewpoint that is not achieved even
in live instruction.

In making this information accessible
in the KNITTING WORKSHOP BOOK, we
want to thank Dan Young for printing our
photographs with such care and skill --
and Elizabeth herself for her willingness
always to do just one more drawing.

Chris and Meg Swansen

ELIZABETH ZIMMERMANN: An Appreciation
by Barbara G. Walker

The first of Elizabeth Zimmermann's writings that I ever read told me how to make a ribbed turtleneck: pick up a multiple of 4 stitches around the neck and work in knit-two purl-two ribbing until you are sick of it.

When I finished laughing, I realized that Elizabeth is more than witty - she's right. Every knitter knows that is indeed how turtlenecks are made.

For many years, I and thousands of other enthusiastic Elizabeth-watchers have heartily enjoyed her wit and wisdom. She's a delight and an inspiration. Her designs are interesting. Her written instructions combine two qualities all too seldom met together: they teach, and they amuse, both at once.

In her goodnatured way, Elizabeth Zimmermann has charmed untold numbers of novices into becoming capable, creative knitters. In her magic world, one learns that a knitted garment is not just an article of clothing. It's an organic growth, compounded of warmth, love, and fun. It's also intellectually stimulating; innovative geometry is Elizabeth's specialty. After becoming

acquainted with Elizabeth Zimmermann
and her work, one almost invariably sees
knitting as among the most entertaining
of human endeavors.

Elizabeth's many devoted fans are sure
to welcome her new publication with
open arms and eagerly poised needles.

- Barbara G. Walker

CONTENTS

2

AFFECTIONATELY
DEDICATED TO
the many devoted knitters
who have participated in
my workshops over the
years, and to you whom
I shall meet through the
video workshops.

4

PART I

BEGINNINGS

A HAT

LESSON ONE

CASTING-ON

AND

KNITTING

This is Elizabeth Zimmermann welcoming you to the KNITTING WORKSHOP. We shall be working all the time, and working through all the necessary and sometimes recondite techniques of handknitting, to the point where you may easily startle yourself at the end by qualifying as a Master Knitter. Some of my tricks may be new to you, and some familiar; but in perhaps a slightly different form. I urge you to consider them all.

FIGURE 1   WOOL-HOLDER or SWIFT

To start with, WINDING THE WOOL. A swift is a beautiful and functional wool holder, and an embellishment to your living-room (see figure 1); but failing it, corral a family member to hold the skein, or even put it round a chair or over your own arms.

To make a CENTER-PULL BALL:

START by winding a few yards round all fingers at once to make a kind of tuft.

THIS TUFT will remain in the heart of the wool-ball, and one end of it will stick out, as you wind, so that when the ball is complete you can pull on the tuft and knit from the center.

THIS IS particularly useful if you are a tight winder, because nothing is worse for wool than stretching. It sometimes stays stretched even

during and after knitting, and then relaxes back
to its unstretched state when washed. You can
easily imagine how this results in a shrunken
sweater.

BUT if pulled from the center, a ball of wool
immediately develops an ever-increasing hole,
and this enables the wool to RELAX from its
stretched state at once.

AFTER completing winding, wind the last yard
or so around the outside of the ball (horizontally)
and TUCK the end in so that a bit sticks out.
How often one wishes one had an extra length
of wool without breaking and joining; well,
here it is.

Let us CAST ON. The most primitive way is by making
a series of backward loops (half-hitches) over the needle
(see figure 2), but these are hard to knit off without
leaving an ever-increasing length of thread between the
stitches.

FIGURE 2 - Primitive
half-hitch casting-on.

Try LONG TAIL CASTING-ON by studying figure 3
and figure 4. If you are courageous, it is not necessary to
start long-tail casting-on with a slip-knot:

LAY THE WOOL over the needle (which is
held in the right hand), with the long tail
nearest you.

FIGURE 3
The first stitch
of Long Tail
Casting-On.

GRASP both pieces of wool with the last three fingers of your left hand.

PUT thumb and finger between the two wools and spread them apart.

PULL the needle down, slip it up next to the thumb, and hook the finger wool through.

Put thumb between the ends and repeat.

MAGIC. The first cast-on stitch will be two stitches. But don't expect this to happen again until you start another casting-on.

WHEN YOU HAVE achieved Long Tail Casting-On, think hard for a minute. What you have just learned is to work the primitive, backward-loop casting-on AND the first knitted row in one fell swoop.

CAST ON about eight stitches, and START KNITTING. You may have noticed that I hold the wool over my left forefinger and hook the stitch through with the right needle. Now you very possibly hold the wool in your right hand and loop it around the needle. Both ways are right, and both yield the same result. They are known as the German or Continental way, and the American or English way respectively. It matters not one bit which you use habitually.

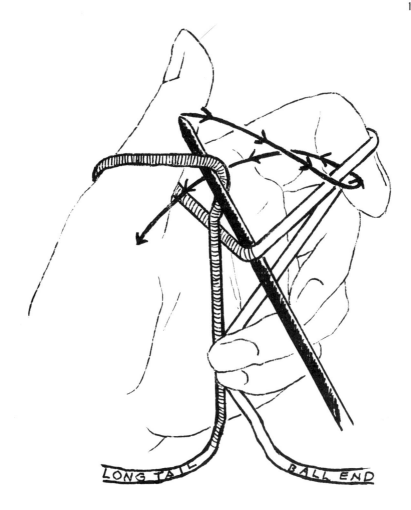

LONG TAIL   BALL END

FIGURE 4 - Although there are at least 7 ways to cast-on, this is the method I invariably use.

I would, however, MOST STRONGLY suggest that you learn both methods, as they will come in very handy later on. On your 8 cast-on stitches, therefore, knit a few rows back and forth. It's a good idea to form the habit of slipping the first stitch of every row in back-and-forth knitting, as this makes any selvedge firm without tightness.

Knitting back-and-forth yields GARTER-STITCH. If you want to achieve STOCKING-STITCH with back-and-forth knitting, you must work alternate rows in purl, because knit and purl are really only two sides of the same stitch. Knit is smooth in front and bumpy at the back; purl is the reverse.

Your intelligence will now whisper to you that if you could continually work the rows in knit, you could attain a smooth fabric without ever purling. Quite right; you could.

AND YOU CAN:

WHENEVER POSSIBLE, work your knitting around and around on a CIRCULAR NEEDLE. All the stitches will have their smooth sides to the front, and you will have NO SEAMS.

Do you really enjoy sewing up seams? No, I thought not. Imagine now, how your knitting life would be improved if you made nearly everything round and round on circular needles: 24 inch ones for the body and shawls, and 16 inch ones for sleeves, hats, and for baby-sweaters.

THOSE ARE THE ONLY NECESSARY LENGTHS. Needles longer than 24 inchs can become rather unmanageable, and the little antique 9 inch and 11 inch ones are practically unusable. I have a whole jar full of straight needles, and they gather dust, because back-and-forth knitting can quite easily be worked back-and-forth on a circular needle. Just practice and see - and no needle will ever have a chance to slide away into the upholstery, or under the car-seat, or, worse, INTO THE DRINK. Search for a circular needle with firm ends, and check to be sure the transition between the ends and the nylon center-section is quite smooth.

TO START YOU OFF on these pleasant paths, I suggest you make a hat on a 16 inch needle, round and round in stocking-stitch. Cast on 72 stitches in a fairly thick wool, working up at a GAUGE of about 4 stitches to 1 inch. Join the end to the beginning, being extremely careful that the casting-on is not twisted on the needle. Start knitting, working the first three stitches with both strands. If you do have a twist, it may be corrected when you come around to the first stitch again; but after that, nevermore.

IF YOU WISH to make a ribbed edge, work in K 2, P 2, and repeat around. This will fit perfectly into 72 stitches. Work the ribbing for about $1\frac{1}{2}$ inches.

QUESTION 1: Which way is the stitch supposed to be on the needle?

ANSWER: If the stitch is regarded as a loop (see figure 5), the righthand side should be in front of the needle (see figure 6A). SHOULD the righthand side be BEHIND the needle (which occasionally occurs with some knitters - see figure 6B), then knit out of it from the back. Try to correct the technique which causes this anomaly in the first place. Actually, it occurs when Continental-style knitters (such as I am), purl the "easy" way, which twists the purled stitch on

FIGURE 5

LOOP

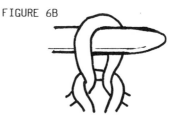

FIGURE 6A

RIGHT SIDE
IN FRONT
"RIGHT"

FIGURE 6B

LEFT SIDE
IN FRONT
"WRONG"

the needle. But this workshop has, at least temporarily, abolished purling, right?

QUESTION 2: WHY DO YOU RECOMMEND WOOL? Easy: wool is warm and comforting, and pleasant to knit with. It is an infinitely renewable resource and does not deplete our oil supply. It looks good. Its sheepish producers are happy to be rid of it for the summer, and will gladly grow a new supply for next year. WOOL ALLERGY, YOU SAY? Well, who ever heard of much wool allergy before the middle of this century, when allergies really came into their own? Could it not come from the dyes or chemicals used in processing wool? Have you ever heard of a sheep allergy? Centuries ago, people had only wool and linen to wear, with silks and furs for the rich, and all they had in the way of allergies was old-fashioned hay-fever. Start a baby off in the very softest baby-wool, and gradually increase the dose to immunize it against this particular allergy (sic), keeping it warm and comfortable at the same time.

Help me down off my soapbox, somebody.

FIGURE 7 - CIRCULAR NEEDLES: These may be strange tools for you. Give them a chance. Like all tools they come in many sizes, qualities, and suitabilities. Don't buy a whole set from a single manufacturer; buy single ones from as many manufactures as you can find, and test them out. LENGTHS: I prefer to use 16" and 24" ones exclusively. MATERIALS: some come in all-plastic, some in metal ends with nylon center-sections. The latter have firm ends, the former bendable ones. MOST IMPORTANT: the joining-point between ends and center-section should be SMOOTH. If it contains the slightest knitsch the stitches may easily catch on it; very annoying and enough to turn you against circular knitting.

LESSON TWO

GAUGE
AND
INCREASING

Do you all have an inch or so of K 2, P 2 ribbing on your 16 inch circular needle without any twisting (see figure 7.) ? GOOD. Are all stitches, both knitted and purled, lying correctly on the needle, with the righthand side of the stitch in front of the needle, both in knit and purl? GOOD.

Ribbing is a bit troublesome to execute, but it has many advantages for a lower edge. First of all, it doesn't curl, as stocking-stitch invariably does; and secondly, it is elastic, and holds in the lower edge nicely. (At the lower edge of a sweater you should work at least 30 rounds for your ribbing to be elastic enough.)

K 1, P 1 RIBBING also does not curl, but it is not so elastic. K 3, P 3 and K 4, P 4 are very amusing, and don't (of course) curl, but they don't hold in nearly as well as K 2, P 2. On a hat we don't need much elasticity, so an inch or so of ribbing is OK. After it, we will increase a few stitches, evenly-spaced around, at a rate of one stitch in--creased for every 6 stitches; this will yield a total of 84 stitches.

72 divided by 6 is 12 ----- 12 EXTRA STITCHES.

INCREASING: Most of you have been taught, I am sure, to increase by knitting into the front and back of a stitch, thus making two stitches out of one. May I suggest that you abandon this practice in favor of MAKE 1 (M 1)?

M 1 is quick, easy, and almost invisible: it is achieved by means of a backward loop (half-hitch) over the right-hand needle (see figure 8), and is knitted into like a regular stitch the next time you come to it.

It is closely related to "pick-up-the-running-thread-between-stitches-and-knit-into-the-back-of-it." In fact they are identical except for the fact that the latter is made out of the previous row.

FIGURE 8

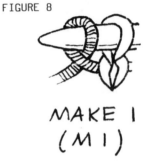

MAKE 1
(M 1)

I think if you make a habit out of M 1, you'll be glad. The loop may be twisted to the right or the left, but be consistent.

When working a pair of increases - for instance one each side of a seam-stitch, twist each in an opposite direction. (see figure 9 ; if you're as fussy as I am, that is.)

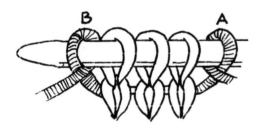

B   A

M 1, K 3, M 1.

FIGURE 9
When meeting these stitches in the next round, K into the front of A and the back of B.

ALL RIGHT: NOW work K 6, M 1 around, (84 stitches) and knit for perhaps 2 inches. Your cap has become some inches bigger; how many inches depends on your GAUGE, and here we come to the KEY-WORD of all knitting.

HOW MANY STITCHES DO YOU ACHIEVE TO 1 INCH WITH GIVEN WOOL AND NEEDLES?

GAUGE

The size of the needle can determine your GAUGE. Your state of mind can influence your GAUGE. In short, GAUGE is an idiosyncratic matter. Some knitters knit more tightly than they purl (or vice versa), so that their stocking-stitch, if worked back and forth, may have alternately tighter and looser rows. In fact, the whole subject is fraught with frustrations. Let us try and simplify it.

FIRST, work as often as you possibly can round and round on a circular needle, and thus avoid the pitfalls yawning for those who knit and purl at different tensions.

SECOND, don't knit when you are in a rage, or tense for any reason. At least, you can knit, but confine this to working on a very tight, strong pair of booddees, or a sock. Keep them in a special place, and take them out only when peeved.

THIRD, test out your GAUGE with given wool each time you start a project.

Did you know that different colors of the same wool may be very slightly thicker or thinner owing to the dying process, and that this can affect your GAUGE?

DON'T test it on a 2 inch square, but on a decent-sized cap. Why do you suppose I'm having you make a cap?

TAKE IT off its needle, lay it out flat, dab at it with a steam-iron, perhaps, and place two pins in it EXACTLY 4 inches apart horizontally. (see figure 10)

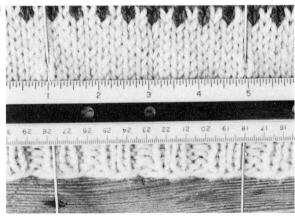

FIGURE 10

NOW, honestly count the stitches (and even fractions of a stitch) between the two pins, and divide them by 4.

HONESTLY.

The result, including half, one-third, and even quarter-stitches, is <u>YOUR GAUGE</u> with this wool and this needle. (If the fractions of a stitch make you nervous, make another swatch on a needle one size smaller or larger, and see if you have better luck. Take a larger needle to get fewer stitches, and a smaller needle to get more.)

NOW, multiply your exact GAUGE by the number of inches you want around your hat or sweater, and the result is the number of stitches to cast on.

A YARDSTICK is more reliable for measuring than a tape-measure.

COUNT YOUR HAT STITCHES again to be sure you have 84, and prepare yourself mentally for some color-pattern knitting in the next lesson.

A plesant way to count your stitches by pairs:

> Two, four, six, eight,
> Mary at the cottage gate,
> Eating cherries off a plate.
> Two, four, six, eight.

Go through this and you've counted off 32 stitches. Twice for 64 stitches, etc.

*   *   *   *   *

QUESTION: My finished sweater is too big. What shall I do?

ANSWER: Surprisingly often the answer is quite simple; just tighten up the cuffs, neck, and lower edge. On the lower ribbing, you may run about 6 rows of elastic thread on the inside, starting a fresh thread with each round. Now, grasp all six threads together and pull them up to fit. Knot the six beginnings to the 6 ends and the body will suddenly "fit".

For a ribbed neckline, run just one doubled elastic thread through it on the inside.

For ribbed cuffs, it is better to rip them and re-knit them on fewer stitches.

WATCH OUT: you cannot rip from a cast-on edge upwards. It is better to snip one stitch at the top of the ribbing, take out one row (or round), unravel the cuff, pick up the stitches, decrease in one round to the necessary width, and knit the new cuff down. Cast off loosely.

Many garments are considered too big only because they are loose at just these above three points. Most people like roomy sweaters with snug edges.

REMEMBER to cast off K 2, P 2 ribbing by knitting the knit stitches and purling the purl stitches.

The above shows how honest we are. This question was really picked out at random during taping of the KNITTING WORKSHOP and does not apply until PART II.

LESSON THREE

COLOR-PATTERN KNITTING

You may not believe it, but you are now far enough advanced to tackle color-patterns, as in ski-sweaters. Once you have grasped the principle, you must admit that they are no more complicated than knit-and-purl patterns.

YOU ALL REMEMBER how I advised you to knit the way you preferred - righthanded (throwing the wool with your right hand) or lefthanded (holding the wool over your left forefinger and hooking the stitches through with the right-hand needle)? I encouraged you to familiarize yourself with both; NOW you are going to see how smart you were to follow my advice.

You are going to put a color-pattern into your 84-stitch cap on the 16 inch circular needle.

CLEAR FROM YOUR BRAIN all injunctions to "Take the new color from under the old color"; and to "Twist the colors every time you change them". Both these commands are absolutely redundant unless you are making Argyll socks, and who makes Argyll socks anymore, thank goodness? They were troublesome and confusing and slow. Good luck to them; let us leave them to fanciers of obsolete fashions. Don't misunderstand; they belong to the Scottish heritage, and if you want to appear in full Highland Fig*, including kilt, sporran, and whatever that thing is that you stick in your stocking**, you should have a pair - more-or-less in your ancestral tartan. Extremely few of us qualify for this.

We are now embarking on two-color Scandinavian patterns, to which two very comforting rules apply:

FIRST: Never employ more than two colors at one time, and view with suspicion any design that would have you do otherwise.

SECOND: Never choose a design that would have you carry one color more than 5 stitches at a time.

LET US START with the simplest of all patterns: alternate stitches of either color. With this you can practice using both knitting methods alternately. Knit fairly loosely; alternate stitches are hard to work tightly anyway. After one round of this, work one round of all pattern-color, and then another round of alternate stitches. You may place the colored stitches directly over those of the first round (see figure 11), or alternate them (see figure 12).

WORK half a round of each of these to see what a

FIGURE 11   FIGURE 12

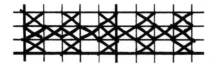   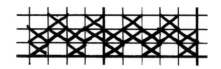

completely different effect this simple change produces. Now work two rounds of background color and try another pattern.

* See Lady Gainford's DESIGNS FOR KNITTING KILT HOSE
                    AND KNICKERBOCKER STOCKINGS.
** Skean Dhu, we believe.

Get out some graph-paper and practice making your own graphs. (You will notice that we use KNITTER'S GRAPH PAPER, which incorporates the correct relationship between stocking-stitch stitches and rows.)

START with the very simplest: reverse the first pattern on the hat by working one round of color, one round of alternate stitches, and a third round of color. I think this will surprise you. It is one of the very prettiest patterns, and also one of the simplest. (see figure 13) Practice making squares, triangles and diamonds, and anything else you wish.

FIGURE 13

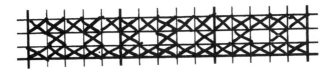

If a pattern calls for a space of more than 5 stitches, place one stitch in the middle of the space; or even a small motif of 2, 3, or 4 stitches. Scrutinize genuine Norse sweaters, and you will find that this device is quite common. WHEN you find - as you sometimes do - more than two colors employed in a single row, you can assume the knitter was so competent that he or she could carry two colors over the left forefinger and the third color in the right hand.

In order to keep a three- four- or five-stitch carry loose, I employ TWO TRICKS which you may like to emulate, or improve upon:

FIRST: When starting the righthand color after 5 stitches of the other color, I pull the knitted fabric to the right and bring up the righthand wool quite loosely for the first stitch, producing a gentle loop across the back. (see figure 14)

SECOND: When starting the lefthand color after 5 stitches of the other color, I hold a modest loop of the new color

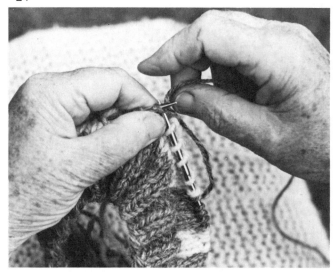

FIGURE 14
When working the
righthand color
after a 4-or-5-
stitch carry, pull
the stitches on
the righthand
needle to the
right, and gently
loop the new
color across the
back.

against the righthand needle while I knit its first stitch. (see figure 15) Thank goodness that the marvel of video enables me to SHOW you this; they are both difficult to describe.

WORK YOUR CAP to a length of 4-to-5 inches, putting in any patterns you please and selecting some with carries of up to 5 stitches. The patterns used in the cap knitted on the video are shown in figure 16.

NEXT TIME WE'LL DECREASE.

FIGURE 15
When working the
lefthand color
after a 4-or-5-
stitch carry, pin
a bit of the new
color against the
righthand needle
with your fore-
finger while you
knit the stitch.

QUESTION: "I measured my husband around the chest. How many inches do I allow for ease?"

ANSWER: When possible, AVOID measuring people around the chest. Find out which is their favorite fitting sweater, and measure IT around the chest.

Some people like snugly-fitting garments; some are happier in something loose. But HOW loose, they have a hard time explaining. The main thing is to have a garment that is snug around the neck, cuffs, and lower edge.

Even if it's TOO snug, the knitting will obligingly stretch. That's one of the endearing characteristics of knitting; it accomodates itself. So make the body fairly - or very - loose, especially at the underarms (wide sleevetops and deep armholes), and persevere with grim determination when working those 30 rounds of ribbing at the beginning.

Of course, you don't invariably have to start with ribbing; some wearers will settle quite happily for an inch or so of garter-stitch border. In this case, cast on fewer -- perhaps 10% fewer -- stitches to start with, and in the first round of stocking-stitch work K 10, M 1 around. We will deal with hems later on.

FIGURE 16
Pattern-graphs
used for the hat
knitted on the
video.

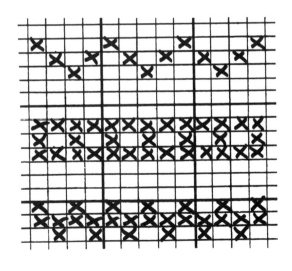

The hat with color-patterns completed and
ready for decreasing.

LESSON FOUR

DECREASING
AND
BLOCKING

MY CAP is now about $4\frac{1}{2}$ inches high, and I'm ready to decrease. I've decided to do this at 7 points around the cap. WHY? Because I'm fond of the number 7; because it's an uneven number; because it's a magic number; and for a very practical reason, because it divides evenly into 84.

The most primitive way to decrease one stitch is by Knit 2 together (see figure 17), and it's still one of the best ways.

FIGURE 17

KNIT TWO TOGETHER
(K 2 TOG)

FIGURE 18

SLIP, SLIP, KNIT
(S S K)

The lefthand stitch of the pair will lean over and swallow up the righthand stitch, and the decrease will lean to the right.

TO SLANT to the left, we usually slip one stitch, knit the next, and pull the slipped stitch over it. Called sl 1, K 1, PSSO. It slants quite effectively to the left, but many knitters notice that when these two techniques are paired, the former presents a smoother appearance than the latter. This annoys them so much that they will go over the completed decrease-line, and, by judicious tightening and loosening, smooth out the sl 1, K 1, PSSO. This is possible, but very time-consuming.

NOW, A WARNING: Some misled people would have you substitute Knit-Two-Together-Through-The-Back-Loops for sl 1, K 1, PSSO.

AVOID THIS; don't try to convince them of their error (it twists both stitches); just smile, and avoid.

TRY, then, THIS: "Slip two stitches knitwise, put the tip of the lefthand needle into them, and knit them together from this position." (see figure 18) Thank you Barbara Walker.

FIGURE 19
Decrease by Knit 2 together to
spiral to the right.

This decrease, which Barbara has succinctly named SSK (Slip, Slip, Knit) is as perfect a mirror-image of K 2 Together as you can possibly achieve, and after one washing IS a perfect one.

ALL RIGHT then: K 2 tog. leans to the right; SSK leans to the left, because they consume respectively the stitches to the right and the left of them. If you consistently use one or the other of them, your decreases will -- on the top of a hat for instance -- spiral to the right (see figure 19) and to the left (see figure 20). If you employ them alternately, the decrease will go straight.

LET'S HAVE our decreases spiral to the right, employing plain old K 2 together.

Knit 10, K 2 together around, and you'll end up with 7 fewer stitches. Work one plain round. Knit 9, K 2 together around, (7 fewer stitches again. 70 stitches now remaining). Another round plain. K 8, K 2 together; 63 stitches. And so on. By now your stitches are rather stretched on the 16 inch needle; put them on 3

FIGURE 20 -
Decrease by SSK to spiral to the left.
Note that this cap has 6 decrease points.

double-pointed needles and work with the fourth needle, and continue thus down to 7 stitches. Pull the wool through them and finish off AS FOLLOWS:

Thread the end through a huge, sharp needle and skim through the back of the fabric. Finish off all ends in this manner.

Your decreases have spiralled counter-clockwise. To make them spiral clockwise, decrease by SSK. To make them go straight, alternate these methods.

(There is a fine decrease which straightens them most gratifyingly: Slip 2 together as if to knit, Knit 1, pass the 2 slipped stitches over. (see figure 21) Repeat this double decrease every 4th round.)

AN IMPORTANT NOTE: When you decrease as above (all three methods), your cap will come to something of a point. In order to flatten the top, speed up the decreasing when you have 7 X 7 stitches remaining (a little more than

SLIP 2 TOGETHER KNITWISE,
KNIT 1, PASS 2 SLIPPED STITCHES
OVER. DOUBLE DECREASE.
(SL 2 TOG, K1, P2SSO)

FIGURE 21

half). Decrease <u>every</u> round from then on, and the top will flatten nicely.

BLOCKING. No trick at all since the invention of the steam iron. Heat the thing up and just dab at your knitting.

NEVER IRON IT. Bulges, caused prehaps by increasing or decreasing, will flatten out with docility when just breathed on by this wonderful contraption.

When ribbing is warm and steamy, pull on it vertically to help it into shape. When storing a ribbed-edge garment always fold the ribbing up.

FOR washing and blocking, see KNITTING WITHOUT TEARS, pages 114-117.

THE COMPLETED CAP

PART II

TWO

SWEATERS

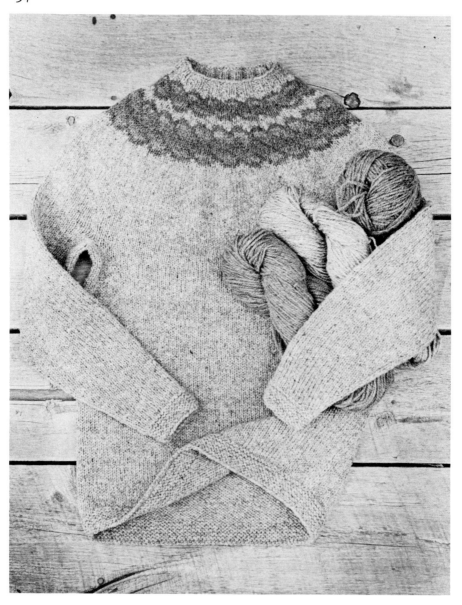

THE HAWSER SWEATER

This sample sweater took four
four-ounce skeins of wool.

LESSON ONE

SEAMLESS YOKE-SWEATER BODY AND SLEEVES

Now that you know the techniques involved, we're actually going to make a garment; a seamless yoke-sweater. REALLY -- no seams at all, unless you count the woven underarms, which will be totally undetectable when completed.

The key word is, as always, GAUGE. I would not dream of dictating what wool you should use, nor at what GAUGE you should work. This is entirely a matter of taste. Fine wool is knitted at a fairly small GAUGE, and thicker wool at a larger GAUGE. Take some wool which suits your fancy and experiment, knitting it up with various sizes of needles.

Cast on 75-90 stitches on a 16 inch circular needle and knit around for 4 to 5 inches. Take out the needle and lay the knitting flat and measure off 4 inches horizontally in the middle. Mark the distance with pins, and honestly count the number of stitches to 4 inches. Divide this number by 4, and the result, including fractions of a stitch, is YOUR GAUGE.

FORMULA

YOUR GAUGE	X	INCHES YOU WANT	=	NUMBER OF BODY STITCHES
($4\frac{1}{2}$)	X	($34\frac{1}{2}$)	=	(156 sts)*

*Actually 155.25 stitches, but we will use 156 stitches for ease of mathematics.

MEASURE the favorite sweater of the person for whom you are knitting, rather than the person itself. (see figure 22) Multiply the inches around the body by your GAUGE, and the result is the number of stitches for the body -- THE KEY NUMBER.

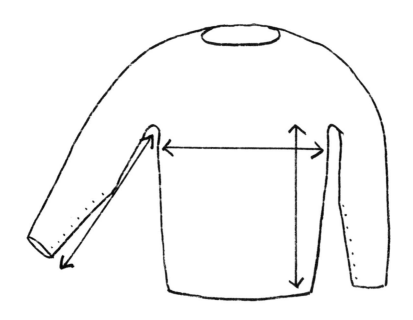

THE 3 NECESSARY MEASUREMENTS:
WIDTH AROUND CHEST.
BODY-LENGTH TO UNDERARM.
SLEEVE-LENGTH TO UNDERARM.

THE KEY NUMBER is 100%, and all other measurements are percentages of it.

BODY. Since the sweater is to have a garter-stitch lower edge, I shall cast on 10% fewer stitches then calculated to hold in the lower edge.

$$10\% \text{ of } 156 = 15.6 \text{ or } 16 \text{ stitches}$$

$$156 - 16 = 140 \text{ stitches}$$

$$(100\% - 10\% = 90\%) \qquad *$$

(I shall increase the needed stitches [16 in my case] after the border, join my knitting, and change to stocking-stitch -- all knit. In fact, I've not purled a stitch yet, and don't plan to until the very end.)

MY HAWSER SWEATER, as knitted on the video series, is $34\frac{1}{2}$ inches around -- for a medium sized child. The body will require 156 stitches, which, once again, is my GAUGE -- $4\frac{1}{2}$ stitches to 1 inch -- times the desired body girth -- $34\frac{1}{2}$ inches, LESS 10% (16 stitches). This equals 140 stitches, which is the number I cast on.

WORK back-and-forth on a 24 inch circular needle for a good inch -- perhaps 6 ridges of garter-stitch.

NOW JOIN, being careful not to twist, and continue around, increasing the needed 16 stitches (10%) evenly-spaced -- about every 9 stitches. DON'T WORRY if the spacing doesn't come out exactly.

INCREASE by the Make 1 method, (see page 16), and the increases will be successfully hidden by the change of fabric.

(You may, of course, work the lower edge in K 2, P 2 ribbing on the same 140 stitches. Ribbing is more elastic than garter-stitch, and you should work at least 30 rounds [around and around] on your circular needle.)

WORK to wanted length to underarm (see figure 22), in my case 15 inches. After about 6 inches, take your work off its needle and HONESTLY measure the width. If it is not wide enough by, say, 8 stitches, these may be increased

* See pages 153, 154 for EPS formulas.

two at a time, at the underarm seamlines:

> With a safety-pin, mark the exact seam-stitches
> -- in my case 77 stitches apart. Work to within
> 1 stitch of the seam-stitch. Make 1, K 3, Make 1.
> Repeat at the other seamline. You've increased
> almost 1 inch. Repeat as often as necessary,
> spaced a few inches apart. (see figure 9).

IF you are knitting for a person with narrow hips and
wide shoulders, you may plan these increases. Start the
sweater with less than chest-measurement, and increase
gradually.

There is a faintly-related technique for making a well-
fitting sweater which is here perhaps appropriate:

> The tendency of sweaters to Ride-Up-At-The-Back
> and Droop-At-The-Front is a knitter's (and a wear-
> er's) bugbear. It can be SUCCESSFULLY COMBATED
> by means of SHORT ROWS, and short rows can be
> tamed into invisibility by WRAPPING .

PAY ATTENTION: The secret is to make the back longer
than the front by occasional insertions of pairs of short rows
placed at regular intervals as needed:

> WORK across the back to within 3 stitches of the
> underarm seam-stitch. WRAP the wool around the
> next (unworked) stitch on the lefthand needle,
> AS FOLLOWS: (see figure 23)

FIGURE 23
This drawing
shows the completed
wrap just prior to
turning and purling
back.

Wool forward, slip next stitch off the lefthand
needle onto the righthand needle. Wool back.
Replace stitch on lefthand needle. WRAP COMPLETED.
Turn. Purl back to within 3 stitches of the other
underarm seam-stitch and repeat for second wrap.
Turn and continue around.

NOW: When you come to the WRAPPED STITCH,
work IT and the WRAP together. (see figure 24)

FIGURE 24

KNIT STITCH AND WRAP TOGETHER

Continue around, and treat the second wrapped
stitch as follows: Slip the wrap, Knit the stitch,
Pass the wrap over, (or SSK). The back is now
2 rows longer than the front. Repeat at regular
intervals as often as wished.

The above technique and the raising of the neckback,
which will come later, can absolutely perfect the fit of
your sweater.

WHEN YOU ARRIVE at the wanted length to underarm
it's time to think about the underarms, which are 8% of the
body stitches. My calculator tells me that this is 12.48
stitches, but I don't let that bother me -- it's MY sweater,
after all -- we'll call it 12 stitches.

AT each side, right above those side-increases, we'll put 12 stitches on pieces of wool, (see figure 25) and leave them to hang there for the time being. Knit across the front to 6 stitches past the seam-stitch; put the just-knitted 12 stitches on a piece of wool; knit across the back; and repeat at the other side.

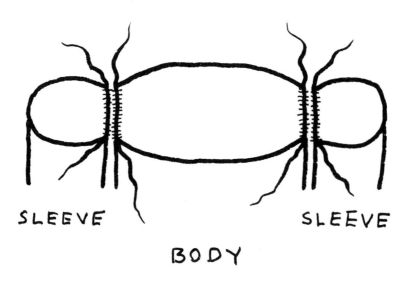

SLEEVE   SLEEVE

BODY

FIGURE 25 - The diagram shows the knitted, circular body-tube with 12 stitches at each underarm on pieces of wool -- aligned with the completed sleeve-tubes, each with a like number of underarm stitches on threads.

BE QUITE PARTICULAR that the front and back have an equal number of stitches, and set the body aside.

START THE SLEEVES

BEGIN with 20% of the KEY NUMBER (body stitches). For ribbed cuffs, use four needles; for a garter-stitch border, use a circular needle back-and-forth, or two needles. After 30 rounds of ribbing or a good inch of garter-stitch, continue around in stocking-stitch.

FEWER than 50 stitches must be worked on four double-pointed needles; but you start increasing right away, and will soon have sufficient stitches for a 16 inch circular needle.

TO INCREASE SLEEVES, use the same method as on the underarm-seams of the body -- Make 1, K 3, Make 1 -- (see figure 9 again). REPEAT this every 5th round, i.e., increase in the first round, work rounds 2 - 5, increase in the 6th round, and so on. KEEP the "seam"-stitches in a strict vertical line, using a safety-pin marker.

When you have increased the sleeve to 33% of the body-stitches, work straight to the wanted length to the underarm; surprisingly often around 18 inches for an adult size. Mine are 16 inches for the video sweater. (A ribbed cuff gives more leeway in arm-lengths.)

FOR A SMALL CHILD, make the sleeves straight, starting right away with 33% of the body-stitches. And be sure to start with generous ribbing to allow for growth.

When the sleeve is long enough, put the same number of stitches as you did for the body (in my case 12) on a piece of wool at the underarm. (see figure 25 again)

MAKE a second sleeve.

PREPARING FOR THE YOKE

Now the bulk of the knitting is behind us, and the fun begins:

KNIT across the front of the body to the stitches of the right underarm.

KNIT the stitches of one sleeve on to the body needle.

KNIT across the back.

KNIT- on the stitches of the second sleeve.

The four blocks of stitches on pieces of wool will match -- if rather untidily -- at the underarms, and knitting continues around on all other stitches.

PHONEY SEAMS

For those who complained that circular sweaters "had no seams" and therefore "didn't hang right", we invented the Phoney Seam, which we've now decided is an indispensible adjunct to a well-made sweater:

FIND the "center-stitch" of the 8% of stitches at the underarms, and drop it clear down to the border or the ribbing of the sweater.

NOW, with a crochet-hook, hook it up again, but with a different relation-ship of stitches to rounds -- two stitches for every three rounds. (see figure 26)

PUT the crochet-hook in the first stitch at the bottom of the runner you've made, and hook the next two threads through it.

THEN hook one thread. Then two, then one, then two, and so on.

P H O N E Y   S E A M

THERE will be 2/3 as many "rounds" for this stitch as for the rest of the fabric which will hump it up slightly to form an ineradicable and good-looking pressed-in seam. This gentle technique will, I think, also eliminate the trauma about dropped stitches forever.

*   *   *   *   *   *

LESSON TWO

YOKE PATTERNS

WEAVING AND

FINISHING

THE YOKE, which is a combining of the body-stitches (100%), plus two sets of sleeve-stitches (33% each), and minus the underarms on both sleeves and on both sides of the body (4 times 8%), is now 134% of the original body-stitches.

$$100\% + 33\% + 33\% = 166\%$$
$$166\% - (4 \times 8\%) = 134\%$$

MORE OR LESS; give or take; we'll not be fussy about an extra stitch or two. This is, after all, knitting, and knitting is elastic by definition. We'll consider the yoke to be one-and-one third of the stitches around the chest.

SO FLEXIBLE is knitted fabric, and so accomodating, that we can knit half the depth of the yoke without any shaping whatsoever. If you wish to put in a pattern with a large repeat, now is the time to do it -- before the decreasing begins -- which might possibly distort it.

COUNT how many stitches you need for each repeat of this pattern, and see if they will divide into the number of yoke-stitches. If they won't go exactly, it is quite permissible to increase or decrease half a dozen stitches (equally spaced) to accomodate the pattern.

(Increasing by Make 1 is almost invisible; decreasing is slightly less so.) (see Part 1, Lesson 4)

WORK about an inch plain before beginning this pattern so that it does not distort where the body and sleeves join.

I am working the first half of the yoke without any pattern, because we rather like the look of a small pattern, having worked so many deep ones.

FIGURE 27

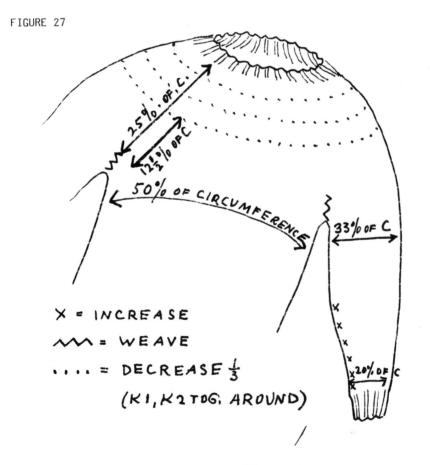

X = INCREASE

∧∧∧ = WEAVE

.... = DECREASE $\frac{1}{3}$

(K1, K2 TOG; AROUND)

THE YOKE will contain three decrease-rounds of K 1, K 2 together, repeated around. This is quite a fast rate -- one third -- but any puckering will disappear with docility when patted with the steam-iron.

RIGHT AWAY, after the decrease-round, I shall start my pattern: THE HORIZONTAL HAWSER. 15 rounds deep, with a repeat of only 6 stitches. (see figure 28 and 29)

It employs four colors, but never more than two at a time, (this is one of my inflexible rules; the other is never to carry the wool more than 5 stitches at a time).

THE HAWSER itself is a beautiful deep pink with blue inside. Can you see on the video how the blue flimmers? This is because I've used three shades of it successively; 2 rounds of pale blue, 2 rounds of medium blue, 2 rounds of plum, and then back through the medium to pale blue.

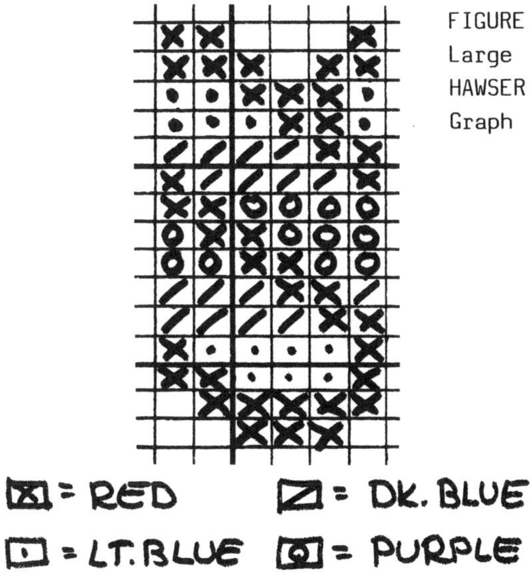

FIGURE 28
Large
HAWSER
Graph

They are so close in tone that at first you don't realize that something lively is going on; but they add depth to the pattern, and help you use up odd bits of wool from your basket.

☒ = RED   ◩ = DK. BLUE
⊡ = LT. BLUE   ◧ = PURPLE

BE SURE to carry the wool loosely across the back of your work, of course, carrying one color in either hand.

When starting the righthand color, I pull the knitting on the righthand needle to the right and knit the first stitch of the new color very delicately, so as to leave a nice loop

across the back. When starting the lefthand color, I take
up a small loop of it with my right forefinger and hold it
against the righthand needle until the first stitch is worked.
(see figures 14 and 15 in Part I.)

YOU may like to use either or both of these methods,
or invent one of your own. The important thing to remember
is that TIGHTLY-CARRIED WOOL DISTORTS the pattern
and makes your knitting puckery and inflexible.

Loosely-carried wool, if TOO loose (very rare), can
always be tightened later; with tightly-carried wool you
are sunk.

(In my experience, carries of only one stitch are quite
easy to keep loose without recourse to the above methods.
This is because neither color is being carried any significant
distance.)

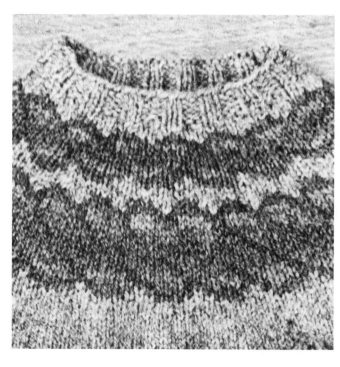

FIGURE 29
A close-up photo-
graph of the
Hawser Yoke.

WHEN THE PATTERN IS DONE, knit one round of background color and then work the second decrease of K 1, K 2 together around.

THE SECOND PATTERN is a smaller version of the first, and has only ten rounds -- partly because the yoke is almost deep enough. (see figure 30)

AFTER completing the second pattern, work one round plain again. Check to see if the yoke is deep enough, and then put in the last decrease-round of K 1, K 2 together around.

FIGURE 30 - SMALL HAWSER GRAPH

Remember, all knitting graphs are started at the lower right-hand corner, and read from right to left.

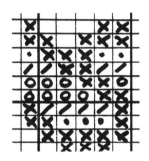

YOU WILL end up, magically, with 40% of the body-stitches, (give or take, of course).

⊠ = RED   ⊘ = DK. BLUE
⊡ = LT. BLUE   ⊙ = PURPLE

NOW comes the very vital BACK-OF-NECK-SHAPING. We will make the neck-back ONE INCH higher at the back than at the front.:

THE SHAPING is worked in K 2, P 2 ribbing, (make sure your number of stitches is divisible by 4) and is worked across the back of the neck. (see figure 31)

MARK the exact side-stitches of the neck.

STARTING at the left shoulder, wrap and turn (see figure 23), and rib across to the right shoulder.

FIGURE 31

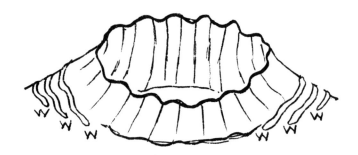

NECK-SHAPING

W = WRAP AND TURN

WRAP AND TURN, and rib back to the left shoulder, PLUS 2 STITCHES.

WRAP AND TURN, and rib back to the right shoulder, PLUS 2 MORE STITCHES.

And so on, for a total of 6 of these short rows.

That's all. BUT VITAL.

CONTINUE around in ribbing for perhaps 4 to 6 rounds, and cast off loosely so that the opening goes easily over the head. (A too-loose neck is easily tightened by running elastic thread around the edge on the inside.)

Casting-Off looks splendid when worked in

CASTING-ON CASTING-OFF:

BREAK WOOL, leaving a long tail to work with, threaded through a large, BLUNT needle.

FIGURE 32

CASTING-ON CASTING-OFF.

WORK FROM LEFT TO RIGHT, and, keeping the wool above, go into the SECOND STITCH from the FRONT and into the FIRST STITCH from the BACK.

PULL wool through, slip stitches off.

GO INTO THE THIRD STITCH from the FRONT and into the SECOND STITCH from the BACK.

PULL wool through, slip stitch off.

And so on.

If you take my advice, you'll take the work off the knitting-needle, and work through the untrammelled stitches with a light touch (and with a BLUNT needle). It's much easier this way, and then you'll see that what you are doing in plain, old OUTLINE STITCH, which any grandma can teach you.

If you still prefer the old tried-and-true casting-off, remember to knit the knit stitches and purl the purl stitches.

ALL THAT REMAINS to be done is to weave the body and sleeves together at the underarms.

DO THIS, also, with a large BLUNT needle; and with another piece of wool.

RESIST the TEMPTATION to use the threads already hanging from sleeve or body.

FACE THE TWO FABRICS to be woven towards each other horizontally.

FIGURE 33

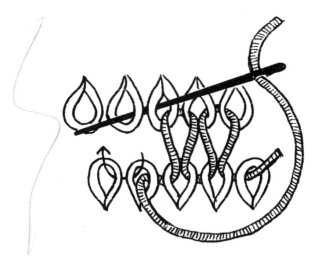

WEAVING, OR GRAFTING, OR

KITCHENER STITCH.

*GO DOWN through the first stitch at the right end of the lower piece, and UP through the second stitch.

PULL the wool through, leaving an end for finishing.

REPEAT from * through the first two stitches of the upper piece.

REPEAT from * on the 2nd and 3rd stitches of the lower piece (remembering to go DOWN through the stitch you came UP through the previous time).

CONTINUE THUS to the last stitches, having the very last stitch go through the fabric of the knitting (twisting this stitch if it wishes to be loose.)

FINISH the other end the same way. DARN in all ends.

TO PERFECT WEAVING, start by coming up through the first stitch on the lower piece, then up through the first stitch on the upper piece, and continue as above.

FINISHING OFF ENDS is a fascinating skill, and one to which I become increasingly addicted:

FIRST, I tie both ends in half a square knot (cross and tuck).

THEN, I split each end into its component plies and DARN IN each ply separately.

USE a large, SHARP sewing-up needle, and skim through the fabric like a spider's web.

This is a most satisfying technique, and especially useful on a sweater that you may one day wish to wear inside-out.

JOIN garter-stitch borders. (see figure 33)

FIGURE 33

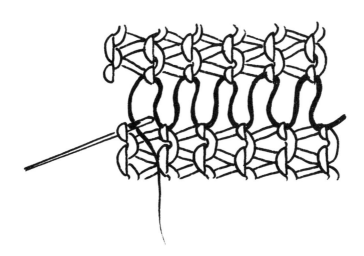

JOINING GARTER-STITCH EDGES.
(PULL FAIRLY TIGHT)

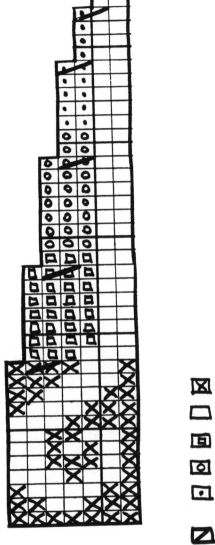

⊠ = BLACKSHEEP
▢ = WHITE
▣ = BROWN
◉ = STEEL GREY
⊡ = SILVER GREY

◪ = DECREASE

FIGURE 34 - MEDUSA YOKE GRAPH.
Work from Right to Left and repeat around. Note the
different decrease method.

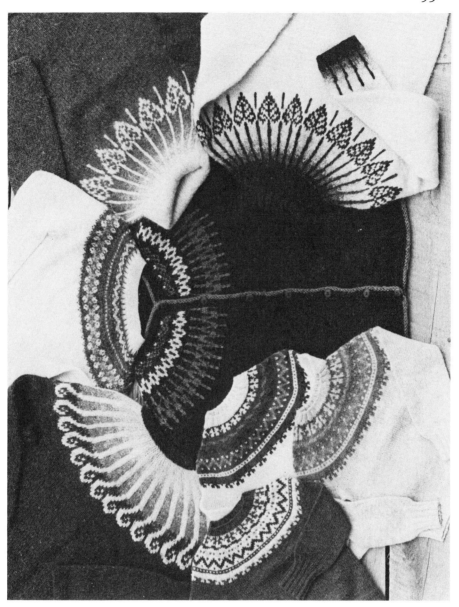

FIGURE 35 - YOKE SWEATERS. Clockwise from lower right corner: THREE variations of SHETLAND YOKE SWEATER (Wool Gathering #11); the MEDUSA SWEATER (see figure 34); FAIR ISLE YOKE SWEATER, (Newsletter # 1); ASPEN YOKE SWEATER, two versions, (Wool Gathering # 7); and, (center), ICELANDIC YOKE SWEATER, (see appendix).

FIGURE 36

THE SHADED ASPEN-LEAF SWEATER
as seen on
THE KNITTING WORKSHOP

LESSON THREE

DROP-SHOULDER SWEATER BODY AND SLEEVES

HERE WE GO NOW with a Scandinavian type of sweater, totally covered with color-patterns.

Having had a taste of this fascinating skill in the yoke-sweater, you now know that it is simple and very rewarding indeed. The possibilities of combining colors and patterns are utterly beguiling and without end.

The Busy Knitter Ski-Sweater was designed as a sampler, as it varies between large and small patterns, all different one from another. The large patterns also alternate heavy and sparse designs. (see figure 37)

FIGURE 37 – THE BUSY KNITTER SWEATER

FIGURE 38 - CLASSIC NORWEGIAN SWEATERS.
These children's Norwegian sweaters are knitted in cream and navy
wool (above), and grey, navy, and a bit of dark red for the
shoulder and sleeve tops (below). See NORWEGIAN KNITTING DESIGNS
for pattern inspiration.

THE CLASSIC NORWEGIAN SKI-SWEATER confines its main patterns to the upper-body and sleeves. It is strictly designed with angular patterns. The body and lower sleeves are either plain or speckled with regular rounds of LJUS (which means lice). (see figure 38)

COLOR-PATTERNED SWEATERS have their origin in the Northern European need for warmth. If you make one in two colors, and carry the pattern-color on every round, it is clear that you've achieved a double-thick sweater at one fell swoop.

OVER THE YEARS, of course, patterns have developed which call for occasional one-color rounds, but basically these sweaters are functional and warm.

THE SHADED ASPEN-LEAF SWEATER

This sweater is one of our own designs (see figure 36), and although the pattern-color stitches are used sparingly at first, you will see that both wools are carried on every round throughout the sweater.

It has another endearing characteristic: its motifs are all separate one from from another, and if you allow the row-change to veer slightly to right and left between motifs (a matter of only six stitches horizontally), you will avoid that disturbing JOG of color at the beginning of every round.

JUST DON'T GET CARRIED AWAY: keep a safety-pin in the actual first stitch of the rounds, and never stray more than six stitches from it.

LET'S START THEN.

Make a circular swatch with the wool you plan to use, putting in a few experimental patterns, and establish your GAUGE, as in the yoke-sweater.

MULTIPLY GAUGE by the wanted circumference; cast on the necessary number of stitches on a 24 inch circular needle, and start right away with the first round of the pattern.

FIGURE 39 - Close-up of the "side-seam" of my SHADED ASPEN-LEAF SWEATER showing the addition of more of the motif on both sides of the seam-stitch as I increase up the body.

(No need to start with 10% fewer stitches as this sweater is provided with a hem, which will hold in the lower edge nicely when the time comes.)

A SWEATER of this kind cannot accomodate short rows to lengthen the back, but it may most certainly be shaped outwards at the sides. Since the pattern-color is employed on every round, it is no trick at all to keep a one stitch line of this color up each side (see figure 39). On each side of this line you will put occasional increases (formed by Make 1, see figure 9), so that the increased stitches are gradually incorporated in the regular pattern.

GREAT FUN. In this case, of course, the line of color will be considered to be the place for changing from one pattern-round to the next.

THE BASIC SHAPE of the motif which is used throughout can be considered a leaf or a tree, or even a heart, if you eliminate the three stitches of the stem and work two plain rounds instead. I prefer to consider it a leaf in honor of a nice ski-resort.

MOTIFS ARE DOVETAILED to fill in space, and subtly shaded to darken the appearance of the garment towards the top. (Or lighten it if you reverse the colors.)

IT STARTS with the outline of the leaf; and then the leaf is gradually filled in with veins, which increase in density, six stitches in each repeat, until there is no more space to insert a single dark stitch without coming up against my anathema: More-Than-Five-Consecutive-Stitches-Of-One-Color!

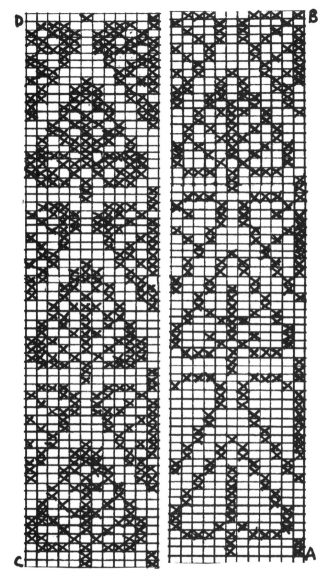

FIGURE 40 –
SHADED ASPEN-LEAF
GRAPH. Work from
right to left.
Start at A, work
to B, then to C,
then to D.
(see appendix)

I did plan to add the stitches six-by-six, but did not anticipate the filling-up of the leaves to coincide so providentially with "desired length for body". That this was superintended by the patron saint of knitting, I am convinced.

FOR THE TECHNIQUES of color-pattern knitting, refer to p. 21- p. 24.

HOLD ONE COLOR in each hand, working the American and the European method alternately, and keeping the carried wool loose across the back.

TOO LOOSE is rare, but permissible. TOO TIGHT is a BANE and a MISFORTUNE.

LET US HOPE that the number of stitches you have cast

on is divisible by the 12-stitch repeat of the aspen leaf. (see figure 40) If there is a small discrepancy, the sweater is allowed to be 2-to-3 stitches wider or narrower. If it is a matter of 6 stitches -- which is a good inch -- you will perhaps choose to use a pattern-colored sideseam-stitch running up each side to accomodate the extra stitches without disturbing the pattern. (see figure 39 again)

WORK TO WANTED LENGTH TO TOP.

BEFORE YOU CAST OFF, it is a good plan to shape the shoulders slightly at the back, particularly in a sweater where patterns do not permit short rows across the back of the body.

SHADED ASPEN-LEAF SHOULDER SHAPING

CAST OFF the stitches of the front and work
across the back to within 5 stitches of the left side.

*TURN and purl back to within 5 stitches of the
right side. (This is naturally troublesome to
achieve, as you will be working the color-pattern
from the wrong side. GRIT YOUR TEETH;
it's not for long.

REPEAT FROM * twice more, and cast off
1/3 of the stitches at either side.

You will notice on the video model that my courage
caved in at this point, and that I worked these short
rows in garter-stitch in the pattern-color; there is
nothing to stop you from doing this too.

FOR A NORWEGIAN NECK, work 5-to-6 ridges of
garter-stitch on the remaining center 1/3 of the
stitches and cast off. For final finishing, see
figure 47 on page 69.

NOW THE SLEEVES

Cast on 20% of the body-stitches, and don't worry about the pattern fitting in; there will be increasing at the underarm so you can run a single-stitch seam-line to demark this, and increase on either side of it.

THE INCREASE RATE is slower than that on the yoke-sweater: 1 stitch increased on either side of the seamline every 6th round; which yields a moderately deep armhole.

MY MIND CHANGES on this subject: On the Busy Knitter Sweater, you will notice a considerably deeper armhole. In this case, I increased every 4th round. Ask the anticipating recipient if a deeper or narrower armhole is preferred. Or again, measure his or her Old-Beloved-Sweater.

WORRY NOT, for when the time comes, the sleeve width dictates the depth of the armhole.

WHEN THE SLEEVE IS LONG ENOUGH, change to pattern-color and cast it off.

You will see that I rather matched mine to the shoulders by inserting a shallow wedge of pattern color and cast off 12 stitches at the beginning of each garter-stitch row, (working back and forth, of course). This is really not necessary, it's just extra detail.

THE TOP OF THE SLEEVE at this rate of increase will be as wide as 1/3 of the body. (On the Busy Knitter Sweater it was 1/2. That patron saint of knitting has been at it again.)

NOW COMES THE ARMHOLE.

BLOCK the finished sleeve with a steam-iron.

LAY THE SLEEVE on the sweater to see where the underarm comes and put a pin there. This is the depth of the armhole.

RUN A BRIGHT-COLORED THREAD down to the pin, keeping a STRICT vertical line. Add another thread at right-angles as in figure 41.

MACHINE-STITCH a row of small stitches down one side of the bright thread, across the bottom, and up the other side. REPEAT, making a second row of machine-stitches.
CUT on the bright-colored basting thread.
(see figure 41)

Now you're in for a GREAT FRIGHT. You will see that the CUT has lengthened. DON'T PANIC. You haven't cut too far. It is a characteristic of stocking-stitch to stretch when it is cut. Calm yourself. You will never fear to cut again.

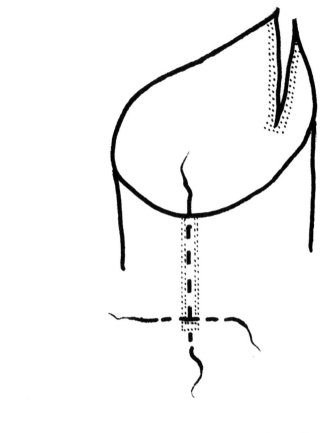

BASTING

MACHINE-STITCHING

FIGURE 41 - CUTTING

In the foreground, the armhole is marked with two basting threads, which cross at the bottom of the armhole. Machine-stitching is then run down, across, and up the other side -- two times for good measure. In the background, the other armhole is shown after cutting, stopping carefully at the point where the threads intersect. Notice that the cut armhole has stretched. DON'T BE ALARMED.

FIGURE 42

KNITTING UP HEM FROM LONG-
- TAIL CAST-ON SELVEDGE.

FOR THE HEM:

FROM THE RIGHT SIDE, knit up a stitch from the back of every cast-on stitch around the lower edge. (see figure 42) You may use finer wool and slightly smaller needles if you like.

KNIT ONE ROUND.

ON THE NEXT ROUND, K 8, K 2 together around for a 10% decrease. (If you did this on the first round, it would give you a KNITSCH every 10th stitch. You may not know what a KNITSCH is, but if you do it you'll find out. It will go hoopty-hoop all around the bottom of your sweater.)

KNIT HEM TO WANTED LENGTH, incorporating name, date, occasion, what you will, in color-patterns. The hem itself may also be in an unexpected color.

WORK THE LAST ROUND in the predominent color of the inside of the sweater, and DON'T CAST OFF.

JUST CATCH EACH STITCH down loosely with the tail of wool. Cast-off edges often look sloppy if loose enough, and bind if too tight. AVOID them where possible.

LESSON FOUR

DROP-SHOULDER SWEATER ASSEMBLY AND FINISHING

PUTTING THE SWEATER TOGETHER

The simplest and one of the best ways to cast off shoulders is in purl -- on the right side -- in standard casting-off, which will form a braid. Shoulders tend to stretch undesirably, and this casting-off keeps them in order.

SEWING THEM UP is then the simplest of the simple:

TAKE THE OUTER SIDES of the two braids
on back and front, and overcast them in
kindergarten fashion. (see figure 43)

YOU MAY take both sides of the braid if
this appeals to you more.

YOU MAY ALSO go in one half-stitch, and out
the next on alternate sides if this appeals to you.

ALL these methods are firm and excellent. Shoulders should be sewn up for about 1/3 of the top, leaving the third third for the neck-opening. Sewing is best worked on the right side.

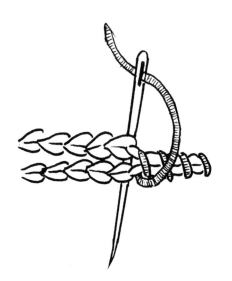

FIGURE 43 –
OVERCAST STITCH.
With a sharp needle,
take the outer
sides of the two
braids on the back
and front of the
body, and work
along.

SEWING UP SHOULDERS

BEFORE YOU SEW IN THE SLEEVES, you should sew an inch or so of the shoulders, then try it on after the sleeves are in to ascertain the correct neck-width.

SEWING-IN THE SLEEVE:

PIN THE BOTTOM of the sleeve to the bottom of the armhole and the top to the top. (Now is where we bend it to our will. We will ease it as in dressmaking.)

PUT A PIN at the halfway mark and one at the quarter-way mark.

TAKE A SHARP NEEDLE for sewing-up. Start at the underarm. There are fewer stitches cast off on the sleeve than there are rounds on the body, so you cannot sew up by counting one stitch for each row.

INSTEAD, find a vertical stitch which will run straight up the body to the shoulder.

FIGURE 44 A -

DON'T VEER. Take
a piece of the body
at this stitch, and a
cast-off stitch of the
sleeve. (see figure
44)

WORK in the color
of the top of the
sleeve, and sew firm-
ly up to the shoulder.

PUT PINS in the
other side and sew
this too.

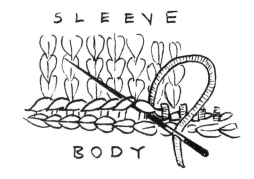

YOU'LL FIND a
certain amount of
fuzz on the inside
which you will snip
off.

FIGURE 44 - SEWING SLEEVE TO BODY.
After pinning to achieve proper position,
start sewing at underarm and work up to
shoulder, following a single, vertical
stitch of the body.

THE CUT EDGE wants to curl towards the body.
DON'T LET IT, or you may have an unwanted
thickness. STEAM IT towards the sleeve and
neaten it with HERRINGBONE-STITCH. skim-
ming the wool across the surface so that it doesn't
show on the right side. (see figure 44 A)

THERE IS A WAY to disguise this seam. It
is a bit thick, and I use it only for sweaters
that I want to be reversible (two sweaters for
the work of one).

FIGURE 45 -
HERRINGBONE STITCH
is used to neaten
the cut edge on
the inside of the
armhole.

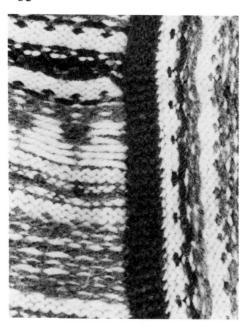

FIGURE 45 - Close-up of sewn garter-stitch strip, knitted in split wool and smaller needles, sewn down over cut edge

I KNIT A LONG STRIP of garter-stitch on about 6-to-8 stitches and apply it neatly over the seam. (see figure 45)

TO HELP PREVENT extra thickness, I split the wool for the garter-stitch strip and use smaller needles.

THERE ARE SEVERAL KINDS OF NECKS:

1. A HEM. From the right side, with possibly a different color, knit up all stitches around the neck-opening, which is roughly 1/3 of the top, on a 16 inch circular needle.

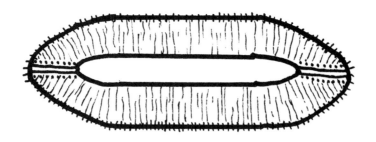

FACED-BACK BOAT-NECK

·······=INCREASE EVERY ROUND

In order to make this hem LIE FLAT, you must increase at enormous speed -- 2 STITCHES AT EACH CORNER EVERY ROUND. (i.e. at the corners, Make 1, Knit the 2 corner-stitches, Make 1.)

CONTINUE for a good inch in stocking-stitch.

WORK the last round in the predominent color of the inside, and sew each stitch down lightly with the same color -- WITHOUT CASTING OFF.

FIGURE 47

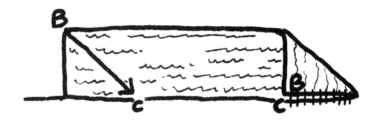

GARTER-STITCH NORWEGIAN NECK.

JOIN B TO C AT EACH SIDE

2. NORWEGIAN NECK. Sew up 1/3 for each shoulder, knit up the center third on the back only, and work a good inch in garter-stitch.

CAST IT OFF and sew the sides of this piece to each end of the neck-front. (see figure 47)

This raises the back nicely as seen in the SHADED ASPEN-LEAF SWEATER. (see page 54)

FIGURE 48

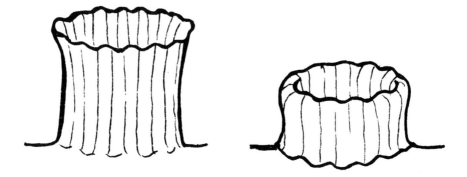

3. TURTLE-NECK. No shaping at all.
Knit up all stitches on a 16 inch needle and
rib until you're sick and tired of it. Cast
off LOOSELY in K 2, P 2.

4. CREW-NECK. A very short turtle-neck
yields a crew-neck. Possibly in garter-stitch.

5. KANGAROO-POUCH-NECK. Scooped out
at the front. (see figure 49) When working
the body, decide where you want the neck to be.

PUT ABOUT 6 inches worth of stitches on a
piece of wool centered at this point.

CAST ON 2 STITCHES (for cutting later)
and continue around, leaving a kangaroo-
pouch.

WHEN YOU'VE FINISHED, run a basting-
thread between the 2 cast-on stitches, machine-
stitch twice on each side of it, and CUT on the
basting. This makes a nice, rounded neck and
is useful on cardigans, in which case its border
of garter-stitch is knitted in one long piece
with the front borders.

FIGURE 49

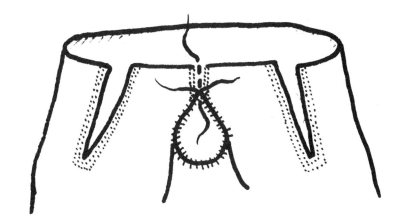

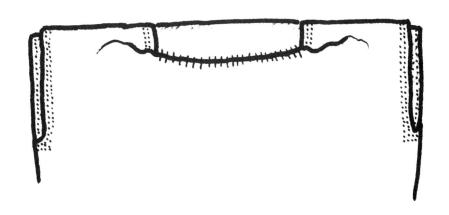

KANGAROO-POUCH NECK.

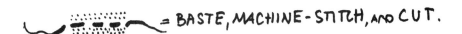 = BASTE, MACHINE-STITCH, AND CUT.

NOTES ON CARDIGAN BORDERS

BASTE, MACHINE-STITCH, AND CUT center-front as for armholes, but, naturally, from top to bottom. (see page 61)

FROM THE LOWER RIGHTHAND SIDE with a smaller size 24 inch needle, KNIT UP 2 stitches for every 3 rounds. (Knit up the 1st and 2nd rounds, the 4th and 5th, the 7th and 8th, and so on.) This gives the right relationship of garter-stitch border to stocking-stitch sweater -- and will neither droop nor pull in. (The wool used may be slightly finer.)

FIGURE 50

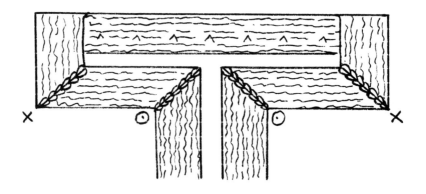

SHAPING OF GARTER-ST BORDER AT NECK.

⊙ = INCREASE 2 STS EVERY 2ND ROW.

X = DECREASE 2 STS EVERY 2ND ROW.

∧ = KNIT 2, KNIT 2 TOGETHER AT HALF-WAY MARK.

AT THE NECK CORNER, mark one stitch with
a safety-pin, and keep this stitch in stocking-
stitch by purling it on the wrong side.

Make 1 each side of this stitch every 2nd row
on the right side. (see figure 50)

YOU MAY make a square neck by reversing this
process at the inner corners. In this case, work
the decrease-stitches as follows:

KNIT to within 1 stitch of corner-stitch.

SLIP 2 together as if to knit, K 1, pass 2 sso.

And talking of cardigans: after 3 ridges of border, work
THE ONE-ROW BUTTONHOLE (from Knitter's Almanac.)

SLIP 1 stitch as if to purl.

Wool forward and LEAVE it there. Slip 1 stitch as if to purl.

PASS 1st slipped stitch over 2nd. Slip 1 stitch as if to purl.

PASS 2nd slipped stitch over 3rd. Slip 1 stitch as if to purl.

PASS 3rd slipped stitch over 4th.

PUT 4th slipped stitch on lefthand needle, REVERSING IT.

REVERSE, twist, or turn the last stitch on righthand needle.
Pull wool tightly, lay it over the righthand needle from front
to back and pull the turned stitch over it.

MAKE FOUR firm backward loops over the righthand needle.

KNIT 2 together, KNIT ON. On the next row, work into the back
of the four cast-on stitches.

FEEL FREE to work short rows once or twice across the
back of the neck for additional shaping.

YOU MAY also K 2, K 2 together across the neck-back
(after 3 ridges of border) to keep the neck from stretching
excessively.

WORK 3 MORE ridges and cast off in PURL on the
right side.

PART III

MASTER

CLASSES

LESSON ONE

SEVEN SEAMLESS SHOULDER SHAPINGS

You have bridged the gulf, and have arrived safely in the MASTER CLASS of sweater design.

By now you are familiar with the necessary techniques of shaping. All you have to do is keep your heads -- and shape in the right places -- to achieve seven seamless shoulder shapings: YOKE, RAGLAN, SADDLE SHOULDER, HYBRID, SHIRT-YOKE, SET-IN SLEEVE and COUSIN NALGAR sweaters.

THEY ALL START as did the Yoke Sweater in Part II: ESTABLISH GAUGE and MEASUREMENT, work body and sleeves, and assemble them on the circular needle, just as you did for the Yoke Sweater.

THEY MAY ALL be stitched and cut down the front to make cardigans as explained in the last lesson, and I think you will agree that the ten minutes courage needed for cutting will soon become ten minutes of smug satisfaction at the mastering of a new skill.

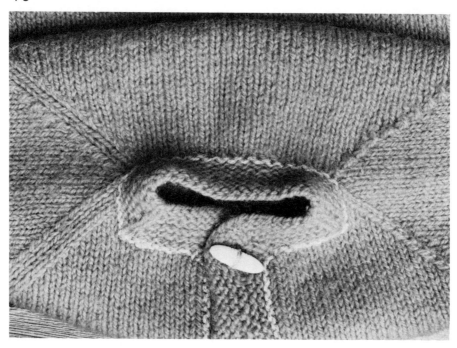

FIGURE 51 - CULLY'S RAGLAN CARDIGAN, seen from a bird's eye view, showing four types of Raglan decreases. Clockwise from lower left corner: 1. K 2 together, K marked stitch, SSK; 2. SSK, K marked stitch, K 2 together; 3. K 3 together, (the second stitch being the marked stitch); 4. Slip 2 together knitwise, (the second is the marked stitch), K 1, Pass 2 slipped stitches over (P 2 SSO).

START ANY OF THESE SWEATERS in the exact same way, and while you are doing the considerable amount of knitting on the body and sleeves, debate with yourself as to how you will end it.

RAGLAN SWEATER

WORK 1 inch after assembling body and sleeves.

MARK the first and last stitches of front and back with small safety-pins, and START DECREASING at these four points.

*WORK to within two stitches of the marked

stitch, KNIT 2 together, KNIT marked stitch, and SSK.

(SSK: "Slip 2 stitches knitwise,
insert the tip of the lefthand needle
into the fronts of these two stitches
from the left, and knit them together from this position." (B. Walker)

REPEAT FROM * at the remaining three marked stitches.

KNIT ONE ROUND.

REPEAT these two rounds for some time. You will notice that the FRONT, BACK and SLEEVES become narrower, as is right and proper in a RAGLAN. (see figure 52)

WHEN the sleeve-stitches are reduced to 10 (for medium-weight adult-sizes sweaters), excluding the decreasing-stitches, it is time to SHAPE THE NECK.

HAVING WORKED the last decrease of the round at lefthand-front decrease-point, KNIT 5 MORE stitches (half of the 10 remaining sleeve-stitches), TURN, and purl back to the right front decrease-point -- plus 5 stitches.

FIGURE 52

FIGURE 53 - Foreground sweater is the RAGLAN shoulder, using K 2 together, K marked stitch, SSK for the double-decrease line. Background sweater is the SADDLE-SHOULDER, showing single-decrease line moving in, then up, then in again to the neck.

PLACE THE REST of the neck-front-stitches on a piece of wool.

REPEAT the decrease-row AND the purl row.

KEEP REPEATING them until the sleeve and un-strung-front stitches have disappeared.

KNIT UP all stitches and work neck border in K 2, P 2 rib for a good inch.

CAST OFF LOOSELY.

SADDLE-SHOULDER SWEATER

MARK FIRST AND LAST stitches on front
and back with safety-pins. Knit one inch
plain, and begin DECREASING.

KNIT to within 1 stitch of righthand front
marked stitch and KNIT 2 together.

KNIT ACROSS sleeve to marked stitch,
SSK (see page 79)

REPEAT across back and other sleeve.

CONTINUE THUS, decreasing EVERY round.

NOW, MEASURE the recipient across his or
her shoulders from bone-to-bone. This is
prehaps 14 inches or so.

MULTIPLY these inches by your GAUGE,
and the result is the number of stitches
needed for the front and for the back.

WHEN, therefore, your front and back have
this number of stitches (including the
decrease-stitches), they are the right
width; and the decreasing, instead of
consuming more body stitches, will start
consuming the sleeve stitches instead.

NOT DIFFICULT. Substitute SSK for
K 2 together, and K 2 together for SSK
at the four decrease points.

KEEP AN EYE on the number of sleeve-
stitches, and when they are reduced to 8%
of the body-stitches (same number as the
underarms), CHANGE the direction of the
decrease back to its beginnings, so that
the sleeves consume the body again.
(see figure 53)

DO THIS FOR 10 ROUNDS ONLY.

NOW COMES THE FIRST SADDLE: on the righthand side knit across the saddle to its last stitch, and SSK.

TURN. PURL BACK on the saddle-stitches to their other last stitch (slipping the first purlwise). PURL 2 together.

TURN. REPEAT these two short rows. I like to slip all first stitches in this manoeuvre knitwise or purlwise as conditions dictate.

WHEN you have worked as many rows as there are saddle-stitches, KNIT (or PURL) your was across to the other saddle and REPEAT this treatment.

NOW COMES THE EXCITEMENT of raising the back of the neck: MAKE a broad, shallow saddle by treating the BACK stitches as you did the saddle-stitches.

WORK back-and-forth on them, consuming the SADDLE-STITCHES until only half of them are left.

WORK AROUND on all stitches (by now you

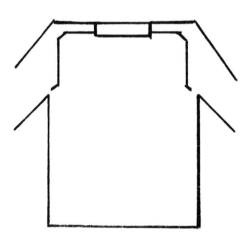

FIGURE 54 –
This decrease line
starts eating up
body-stitches, then
sleeve-stitches,
and finally more
body-stitches
before saddling
up.

SADDLE-SHOULDER

are, of course, on a 16 inch needle) for a good
inch. PURL 1 ROUND and finish with about 1
inch of hem, perhaps on finer needles; perhaps
in different-colored, finer wool. IF THIS IS TO
BE a cardigan, omit the final inch.

THE HYBRID SWEATER

THE HYBRID is very like the saddle-shoulder except
that the armhol seams slant rather like a Raglan and the
saddles are wider:

AT THE UNDERARMS on the body and sleeves
put only 5% of body-stitches on pieces of wool.
WORK 2 ROUNDS.

MARK 1st and last stitches of front and back as
on the Raglan, and WORK a double-decrease at
these points, every THIRD round instead of every second:

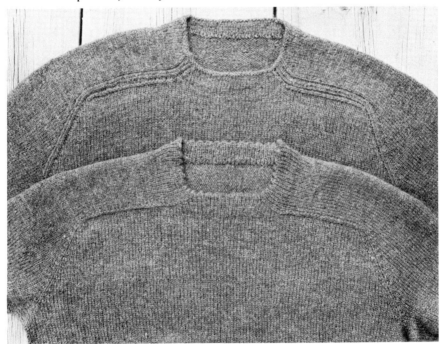

FIGURE 55 - Foreground; front view of the SHIRT-YOKE shoulder.
Background; front view of the HYBRID shoulder.

84

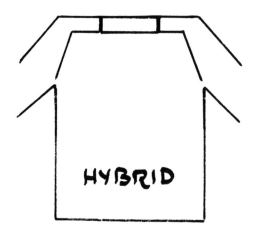

HYBRID

FIGURE 56 -
The decrease
starts like a
RAGLAN, and
ends up rather
like the
SADDLE-
SHOULDER, thus
the HYBRID.

WORK to within 1 stitch of marked stitch, Slip 2 together knitwise, Knit 1, Pass the 2 Slipped Stitches Over.

REPEAT every third round until the sleeve stitches have been reduced to half their original 33%

WORK BACK & FORTH on these saddle-stitches as you did on the Saddle-Shoulder until 1/3 of the front, and of the back body-stitches have been consumed.

KNIT (or Purl) your way across to the other shoulder and REPEAT.

MAKE the center-back "saddle" and the neck finishing as you did on the previous sweater.

THE SHIRT-YOKE SWEATER

THE SHIRT-YOKE is identical to the HYBRID until you have made the first saddle.

THEN, CAST OFF the front-half of the saddle-stitches and continue across the back, decreasing ONLY at the back-body edge. (see figure 57)

FIGURE 57 - Starting like a Raglan, the decrease turns to allow a very deep saddle which continues across the shoulders behind the neck opening.

SHIRT-YOKE (BACK)

WHEN 2/3 of the back-body-stitches have been consumed, BREAK THE WOOL.

MAKE the other saddle, and WEAVE the back-halves together.

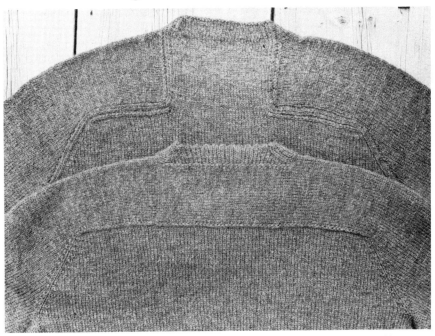

FIGURE 58 - Foreground; The SHIRT-YOKE shoulder viewed from the back. Background; The HYBRID showing the back of neck treatment.

FINISH as on the SADDLE-SHOULDER.

I very much enjoyed continuing the decreases of the saddle up the neck-border. YES: there is_ what the Germans call a SCHOENHEITSFEHLER (a beauty-blemish?) at the end of the yoke-weaving, but this is one of the FACTS OF KNITTING:

> When two pieces of fabric meet
> HEAD-ON to be woven, they will
> always be half-a-stitch off.

Even Mary Thomas can't avoid this.

THE SET-IN SLEEVE SWEATER

THE SET-IN SLEEVE was pigheadedly designed to show that it CAN be made on a circular needle. IT CAN, and very nice it looks, too.

> MARK the 1st and Last sleeve-stitch, and
> have them consume the body (as in the
> SADDLE-SHOULDER) by one stitch every
> round.

> WHEN the body-stitches have been reduced

SET-IN
SLEEVE
(V-NECK)

FIGURE 59 -
Here, the decrease starts eating up the body-stitches to desired shoulder width, then turns to eat up the sleeves all the way to the top.

to shoulder-width, change the direction of the decreases, having the body consume the sleeves, but ONLY EVERY 2ND ROUND.

WHEN there are half of the original upper-sleeve stitches remaining across the shoulder, SPEED UP the decreasing to EVERY round.

WHEN ONLY 10 stitches remain, WORK back-and-forth on the front only, decreasing 1 stitch at the end of each row.

WHEN 5 stitches remain, WORK over to the back and REPEAT the foregoing.

NOW WORK back-and-forth on the back, leaving 3 stitches on the needle at the end of each row, -- and WRAPPING. (see p. 38.)

WHEN 1/3 of the back-stitches remain, WEAVE the shoulders (see p. 50), and finish the neck with a hem or with a garter-stitch border.

If you want to complicate matters with a V-NECK, I refer you to my Wool Gathering #12. The techniques are simple, but would gum up directions for your first circular set-in sleeve to an intolerable degree.

THE NALGAR SWEATER

We call him COUSIN NALGAR because, although technically a seamless From-The-Bottom-Up sweater, he behaves in a very odd way from the underarms on; He INcreases instead of DEcreases, and the sleeves are worked downwards. (see figure 60.)

He's rather a Fitz*, and his name represents RAGLAN spelled backwards.

*
  JAMES II's "NATURAL" (illegitimate) children were given surnames of Fitz -- from the French "fils", meaning son -- followed by the Mother's name.

FIGURE 60 - In the rear, a SET-IN SLEEVE construction with a V-NECK finished in garter-stitch border. Up front, a NALGAR, showing the incorporation of color-patterns during the shoulder and sleeve shaping, one of the organic bonuses of this design.

TO BEGIN THE NALGAR, MAKE a body only, and don't put the 8% of stitches on pieces of wool.

JUST MARK THEM with safety-pins and WORK an INCREASE (Make 1) each side of these marked stitches -- every SECOND round.

CONTINUE around on the swiftly-INcreasing number of stitches until the "underarm" stitches amount to 40% of those you originally cast on.

LEAVE all other stitches to rest, and WORK around the 40% on a 16 inch needle to elbow-length. THEN DECREASE 2 stitches every 5th round to wanted sleeve-length.

REPEAT for the other sleeve.

FRONT AND BACK are then WOVEN together except for 40% of the original body-stitches, which are finished for the neck.

IF YOU LIKE, you may raise the back gently as you did for the SKI-SWEATER on p. 69.

VALUABLE NOTE REPEATED on double Make 1 increases:

> If you twist each one in the oppo-
> site direction with one or more stitches
> between, it gives you perfect shaping. (see p. 16)

I remind myself to make the first twist over my index finger and the second over my thumb, but you may discover a different mnemonic.

FIGURE 61 - Double-increasing instead of -decreasing at the underarms carries the stitch-line up and out, while simultaneously forming the stitches the sleeves will be knitted down on.

LESSON TWO

GREAT GARTER-STITCH

Now we go into a total GARTER-STITCH PHASE. This subject alone would be enough for a book. But I will be just touching the highlights, and am going to refer you to my other publications for further projects.

I would like you to consider using this fabric quite often; it is a beautiful one.

NO PURLING; just back and forth in lovely KNIT. It never curls at any of its four edges. In short, NO PURLING, NO CURLING.

It has a wonderful mathematical characteristic:

Ten ridges of garter-stitch (20 rows back-and-forth) measure EXACTLY the same as ten stitches.

Thus, corners may be knitted at an exact 90 degree angle, (made up of two 45 degree triangular sections), a thing which cannot be achieved -- as you surely know -- in any knitted fabric based on stocking-stitch.

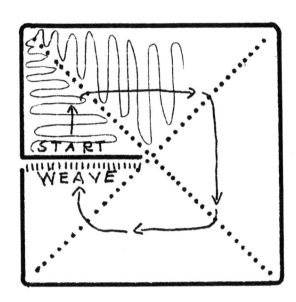

FIGURE 62 –
Start at 9:00
o'clock, decrease
to 10:30, turn
and increase to
12:00, decrease
to 1:30, turn and
continue thus
through 3:00,
4:30, 6:00, 7:30
and the last turn
to 9:00.
WEAVE.

BABY BLANKET

LET US KNIT four 90 degree turns. A . . . .

SQUARE BABY BLANKET.

It is made all in one piece, with just one invisible join.
Decide how wide you want it to be, multiply by your GAUGE,
and:

CAST ON HALF the stitches only.

*KNIT to the last stitch, leave it on the
needle, TURN, and knit back, slipping
this -- and all -- first stitches.

KNIT to the last TWO stitches, TURN,
knit back.

KNIT to the last THREE stitches, TURN,
knit back.

I will stop here, but you don't; just
KEEP KNITTING, one stitch fewer
every second row, and soon you will
observe the beginnings of the first
TRIANGLE.

WHEN the triangle is almost complete,
with about 5 stitches left, start
KNITTING ONE MORE stitch every
second row. (It doesn't pay to work
down to the last stitch, as this gives
the blanket inelegant corners.)

WHEN you are back to the number of
stitches with which you started, ONE-
QUARTER of the blanket is done.
(Get out the scales, and determine
if you have 3/4 of the wool you are
using LEFT. . .)

REPEAT FROM THAT * back there,
and repeat AGAIN and AGAIN.

THE BLANKET IS DONE. It hardly
needs blocking, it is so flat and so
square.

WEAVE the beginning to the end, having
taken out the casting-on on the former.
In fact, if you are aquainted with
INVISIBLE CASTING-ON, this is a good
place to use it. (see KNITTING WITHOUT
TEARS, page 21, or KNITTER'S ALMANAC
page 144)

ONE NOTE on the weaving of garter-stitch: The ROWS
must be in the right relationship to one another. When the
needles are held together, the RIDGE must be up against one
needle, and the VALLEY (between ridges) up against the
other. You then thread the wool DOWN-AND-UP through the
ridge, and UP-AND-DOWN through the valley. Hard to ex-
press; I'll do a drawing. (see figure 63)

GET IT RIGHT; it's worth it.

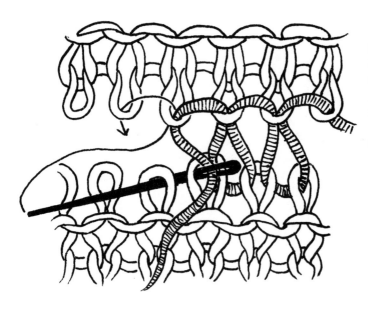

FIGURE 63 –
Garter-stitch
weaving used for
joining the be-
ginning to the
end of the BABY
BLANKET.

Note how the
ridge (bottom)
is being woven
to the valley
(top).

THE PELERINE - 1-ply Icelandic wool,

is STARTED AT THE NECK with 63 stitches and
worked downwards with 3 DOUBLE INCREASES
every second row; one at the center back, and
the other two 1/6 of the stitches in from either
end.

WORK IT for as long as you like.

This will give you a nicely-draped, not too
voluminous cape.

YOU MAY sew up 2/3 of the center-front
if you like.

IF YOU START at the lower edge with hundreds
of stitches and work up, you may have trouble
keeping the double-DEcreases in order at the
beginning. Either way, mark the three shaping
lines with safety-pins.

FIGURE 64 - Above, the PELERINE in single-ply Icelandic wool.
FIGURE 65 - Below, the PELERINE diagram of increase points.

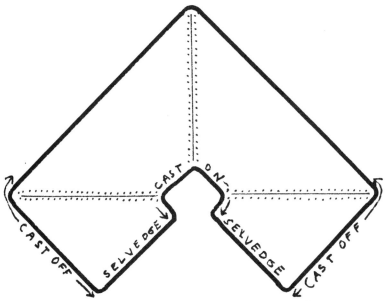

FIGURE 56 -
CULLY'S EPAULET
SWEATER, features
the knitted-in
pocket and the bent-
elbow. Note the
epaulet shaping
across the top, and
the I-Cord borders
with flat buttonholes.

FIGURE 67 -
LLOIE'S JERKIN
is cast on at the
lower back, worked
up and over the
shoulders, and
separated for the
neck and fronts.
Its simple con-
struction makes it
a good beginner's
project.

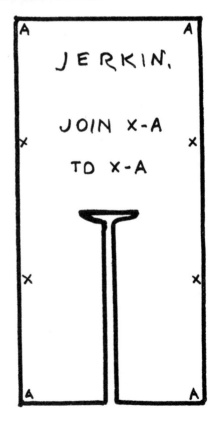

JERKIN,

JOIN X-A

TO X-A

LLOIE'S JERKIN

Is the simplest of the simple, knitted in doubled ICELANDIC wool.

CAST ON for the back and WORK straight.

AT shoulder-length, DIVIDE, having 1/3 for the neck and 1/3 for each shoulder.

WORK about $2\frac{1}{2}$ inches on each shoulder piece (for the neck), CAST ON 1/6 for neckfront, and knit down to match back length.

MAKE other side-front to correspond. YOU MAY want to include a few short rows in the back-shoulder section to give a slight shoulder-back-of-neck shaping.

FOR the endearing I-Cord border, see the end of the lesson

FIGURE 68 -
If you want side slits like those shown here, don't sew the JERKIN seams all the way to the bottom. All edges are then highlighted with I-Cord which is worked last in contrasting-color wool.
Also, a handsome belt may be added by working about 50 inches or so of 3-stitch I-Cord.
You may have noticed the needles in the fabric at the lower left. This is where Elizabeth snipped a stitch as we were taping the video, and demonstrated the After-Thought-Pocket. (see figure 80)

FIGURE 69 –
THE RORSCHACH
SWEATER in 3-ply
Sheepswool.
On the left is a
straight sleeve,
and on the right
a tight cuff.
Pick your favorite.

THE RORSCHACH SWEATER

For the RORSCHACH, I commend you to the appendix. It's a bit complicated. To give you a brief rundown:

It's constructed in TWO PIECES; righthand front-and-back, and lefthand ditto.

The right-angled corners (4 of them) at each neck-side are formed by double-decreasing and/or increasing every second row, and the colored stripe follows the shaping angles.

RIGHT-ANGLES, of course; this is my beloved garter-stitch. The SLEEVES are integral and have some fascinating shoulder-shaping.

THERE ARE TWO cuff-treatments:
IF YOU WANT a Bell-Sleeve, just knit straight and it will bell out naturally.

FOR THE SNUG CUFF, 5 inches shy of wanted length, Knit 2 together across. (see figure 69)

THE BUTTONHOLE TABS
are ours and may be used
on any cardigan or jacket.
(see page 107)

Here is a MYSTERIOUS
I-Cord belt which you may
like to try:

CAST ON 7. * K 4, wool
forward slip 3 purlwise.
Repeat from *.

Startle yourself.

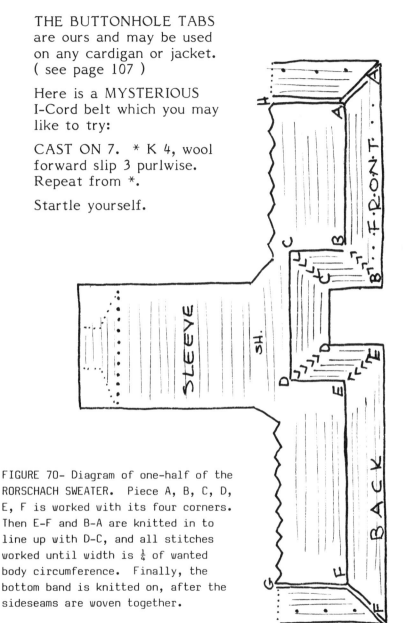

FIGURE 70- Diagram of one-half of the
RORSCHACH SWEATER. Piece A, B, C, D,
E, F is worked with its four corners.
Then E-F and B-A are knitted in to
line up with D-C, and all stitches
worked until width is ¼ of wanted
body circumference. Finally, the
bottom band is knitted on, after the
sideseams are woven together.

THE SURPRISE JACKET

I call it the SURPRISE JACKET because it looks like nothing on earth when you have finished knitting it. Sew up two seams, and you find you have the nicest little garter-stitch baby-sweater or adult mind boggler.

IT IS REVERSIBLE and has no side seams or armhole seams to look ill-fitting or feel uncomfortable.

For specific directions for the Baby Surprise Jacket, I refer you to the Appendix, p. 157. It was designed on vacation and puzzles me to this day. ALL GARTER STITCH. All in ONE PIECE. (see figure 71)

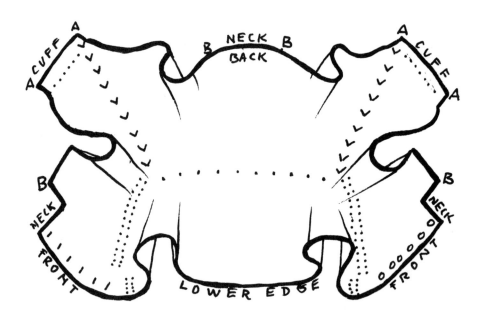

FIGURE 71 - THE SURPRISE JACKET diagram shows the completed garment, all in one piece, before folding to reveal the body and sleeves.

Use up bits of all your old wools -- and only two upper-sleeve-and-shoulder seams to sew up.

EVER SINCE 1969, I've been fighting the problem of giving it adult proportions, and in 1980 I finally achieved it.

THE SECRET is that if you knit up stitches along the WRONG side of garter-stitch long-tail casting-on, you will make an absolutely undetectible join -- from which you may work smoothly down in the opposite direction.

BUT ONLY IN GARTER-STITCH.

FIGURE 72 - ADULT SURPRISE JACKET knitted in every color I could find in my knitting basket. (see News-letter Spin Off #1)

FIGURE 72A-
CHILD'S SURPRISE JACKET. The upper version is shown in the unfolded state, as in figure 71. The striped version shows what the upper mystery will become after sewing up the two shoulder seams.

THE TOMTEN JACKET

The little old TOMTEN JACKET (yes, Swedes, I know that the "en" is redundant) is getting on for 44 years old; the age of our oldest child, although all three of them wore it. We have perfected the pattern a bit to make it MODULAR: All operations in the construction of this sweater are fractions of the number of cast-on stitches, which should optimally be divisible by <u>8</u>.

The prototype is done on 112 stitches, and by varying wool thickness and needle size, (and by using your brains) can fit from baby to slender adult.

CAST ON sufficent stitches (X) for lower edge,

KNIT to wanted length to a DEEP armhole.

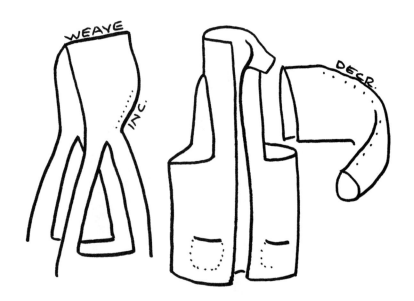

FIGURE 73 - TOMTEN JACKET; at left with hood, at right with collar.

Knit 1/8 of X, cast off 1/4 of X,
knit 1/4 of X, cast off 1/4 of X.

ON the final 1/8 knit twice as many ridges
as it has stitches. KNIT an equal number of
ridges on the other 2 sections. (see figure 74)

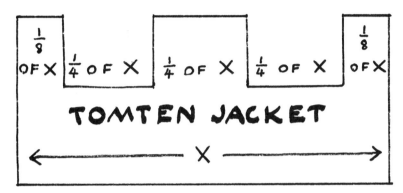

PROPORTIONS FOR ARMHOLES

CONTINUE on all stitches together, increasing,
(for HOOD), 2 stitches at center-back every
2nd row, 8 times. The number of increase pairs
is equal to 1/14 X.

AT 28 RIDGES (1/4 of X), KNIT to the
center and WEAVE together in garter-
stitch weaving. (see page 94)

KNIT UP 1 stitch for each ridge up and down
the deliberately generous armholes and KNIT
for 1/8 of X ridges.

DECREASE 2 stitches at center every 3rd
ridge until 1/4 of X stitches remain.

CAST OFF, and sew sleeve-seam. Zipper, if you
must, and when the baby is quite young, knit a soft,
white hood-lining and sew it in. A twisted cord
can be threaded between it and the hood proper
so the hood can be snugged around the infant face.

Cords threaded through the cuffs eliminate the need for mittens, too. For AFTER-THOUGHT POCKETS, see page 108.

THE RIB WARMER

The RIB WARMER is another Rorschach, now over 25 years old. Approximate GAUGE, 4 stitches to 1 inch.

CAST ON 10 for neckback and KNIT 10 ridges.

CAST ON another 20 stitches and KNIT 40 ridges.

TURN CORNER: Starting at the long edge, K 29, TURN, knit back, K 28, TURN, knit back, and so on down to 15 stitches.

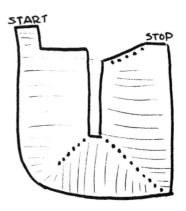

NOW KNIT 1 MORE every 2nd row until you have 30 stitches again.

KNIT 10 RIDGES.

TURN SECOND CORNER, but down to FIVE stitches and back.

FIGURE 75 – The RIB WARMER, in 3-ply Sheepswool, is made in two pieces and joined at the center back. Fits most average adults.

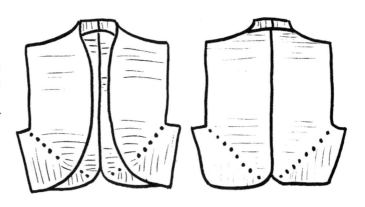

KNIT 35 ridges.

STARTING at the short side, cast off 4 stitches.

REPEAT THIS every second row until 10 stitches remain. CAST them OFF.

SEW shoulder-seams, and beginning-tab to neck-back.

MAKE other half; NO WORRY about the mirror image; this is GARTER-STITCH.

JOIN at center-back.

Hats are the best bazaar-items, but RIBWARMERS come second.

I-CORD

I-CORD is not an unknown technique, but its application has, so far, been little-developed. It can form an effective and convenient edge for garter-stitch projects.

TO START with the cord itself:

ON DOUBLE-POINTED needle, cast on 3.

*KNIT 3.

DO NOT TURN, but SLIDE the 3 stitches to the other end of the needle and REPEAT from *.

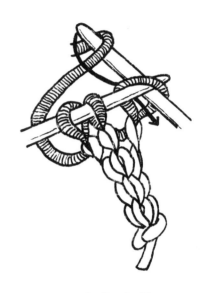

I-CORD

WHAT you are achieving in a minimal piece of circular knitting -- a tiny tube. (see figure 76)

YOU MAY attain the same tube at the selvedges of a piece of garter-stitch:

KNIT to the last 3 stitches, Wool Forward, slip 3 as if to purl. TURN.

REPEAT THIS ROW.

Those last 3 stitches will curl over and form a tube all by themselves.

TO CAST OFF IN I-CORD: Cast on 3 stitches at the end of the row, *Knit 2, slip the 3rd, knit 1 from the final row of the project, PSSO.

REPLACE the 3 stitches on the lefthand needle and repeat from *.

An I-CORD border in a contrasting color is good-looking and decorative:

WITH a smaller needle, pick up the knot at the end of each ridge of garter-stitch; cast on 3, and work as for casting-off.

THIS WILL WORK for the lower cast-on edge too.

When turning an OUTER corner, work two rows (rounds) of I-CORD blind (without attaching it to garter-stitch edge).

To make a FLAT BUTTONHOLE: Work 3-to-4 rows of I-CORD blind, and skip 3-to-4 ridges of selvedge.

To make a LOOPED BUTTONHOLE, work perhaps 9 rows and skip no ridges. The loop may be twisted and secured, or simply tied tight without twisting. (see figure 77)

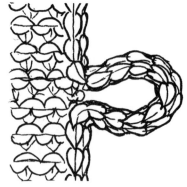

FIGURE 77 - I-CORD BUTTON LOOPS can be tied, or twisted and tied, or left untied.

I-CORD TAB BUTTONHOLES:

CAST ON 3 and work 10 rounds of I-CORD.

TAKE OUT the cast-on stitches and put them on the needle fo form a LOOP.

KNIT 3 RIDGES of garter-stitch on the 6 stitches.

DO NOT CAST OFF; sew skillfully to appropriate side. (see figure 78)

FIGURE 78 - I-CORD TAB BUTTONHOLES, as seen on the Rorschach sweater.

*   *   *   *

THE HEART HAT

The HEART HAT is knitted in garter-stitch and bordered by I-CORD. It also has ties made with I-CORD. (see appendix for complete instructions)

Also refer back to LLOIE'S JERKIN in figure 68 for a good example of I-CORD used for border and ties on a sweater.

N.B. I-CORD will not work as an edge for stocking-stitch.

FIGURE 79 - THE HEART HAT.

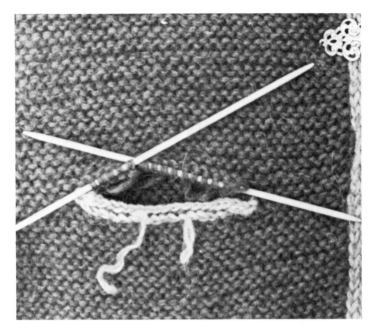

FIGURE 80 - THE AFTERTHOUGHT POCKET, seen after snipping a stitch, unraveling, and placing stitches of the upper edge on needles, ready to knit down to make the pocket. The lower edge has been picked up and cast-off in I-CORD.

AFTERTHOUGHT POCKET

FIND ONE THREAD at the point where <u>you</u> want the pocket, and SNIP IT.

DON'T HAVE HEART FAILURE. Start unraveling the thread in either direction until the resulting opening is as wide as <u>you</u> want for the pocket.

PICK UP STITCHES above and below the opening. THE UPPER ROW will be knitted down for the pocket, INCREASING at the sides, and sewn to the bottom edge of the sweater.

Make the POCKET a little bit shorter than the actual fabric of the sweater because otherwise it tends, when you put things in it, to hang out below the bottom of the sweater.

THE LOWER ROW will be the outer edge of the pocket -- knitted in a contrasting color if desired -- or cast-off in I-CORD. (see figures 80 & 81)

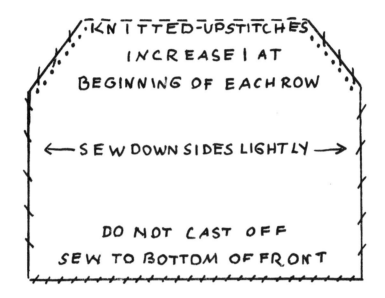

KNITTED-UPSTITCHES
INCREASE I AT
BEGINNING OF EACH ROW

←—SEW DOWN SIDES LIGHTLY —→

DO NOT CAST OFF
SEW TO BOTTOM OF FRONT

KNITTED-IN AFTERTHOUGHT-POCKET

FIGURE 81 - Shows the shaping of the AFTER-THOUGHT POCKET from the inside.

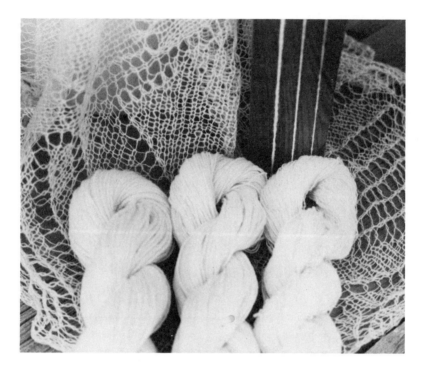

FIGURE 82 - From left to right: Jumper-weight Shetland wool,
Lace-weight Shetland wool, Gossamer-weight Shetland wool.
In the background is a lace veil knitted with Gossamer-weight.

LESSON THREE

LACE SHAWLS

The thinnest wool I know is called Shetland Gossamer or Featherweight; it is practically un-knittable-with. It must be of this wool that the legendary wedding veils were made which, we are told, could be pulled through a wedding ring. This one (see figure 82) goes quite easily through my wedding ring.

But the wool is so VERY THIN that it tends to cling to things and doesn't drape well -- so a once-in-a-lifetime wedding is perhaps what it is best for.

Slightly LESS THIN is the regular Laceweight Shetland, which is very useful for shawls; a 54 inch square shawl weighs not quite 8 ounces. This comes in three shades: white, natural silver, and natural beige. The Scots do dye Laceweight, but in rather crude colors.

Regular JUMPER WEIGHT Shetland also makes splendid shawls and comes in 29 really beautiful colors. It is in this wool that the Fair Isle Sweaters in the next lesson are knitted; splendid colors with intoxicating names like Moorit, Ghillie Green, Loch Maree, Tartan, Bressay Blue, Lovat, etc.

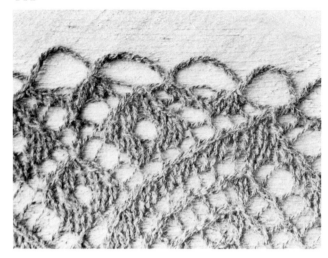

FIGURE 83 –
A CROCHETED EDGE
on a shawl in-
spired by
Marianne Kinzel.
When blocking,
the loops are
individually
pinned to make
a uniform edge.

MUCH DEPENDS on the color and weight you want for your shawl. You may work a shawl in any way you please; the looser you knit, the larger and lacier the shawl will be. If you work tightly, you end up with a kind of doiley.

Needless to say, the CIRCULAR NEEDLE is the obvious tool for shawls.

THE PI SHAWL

The SIMPLEST of all shawls is the PI SHAWL, (see figure 85). Governed by Pythagoras' discovery that a circle doubles its circumference in an itself-doubling series of increases, each of which is twice as far apart as the pre-ceding doubled space. SIMPLE, huh? Ask a mathematician.

THE FOREGOING MEANS:

START with Emily Ocker's beginning:

> MAKE A CIRCLE of wool and
> CROCHET 9 single-crochets into it.
> DIVIDE these 9 on three needles.
> KNIT 1 ROUND.
> (The video is very helpful here.
> This is the spot where all my
> needles hit the floor as I was
> trying to do this manoeuvre.)

EMILY OCKER'S BEGINNING.

FIGURE 84 –
EMILY OCKER'S
BEGINNING for
shawls enables you
to form a neat
center circle,
which may later
be drawn closed.

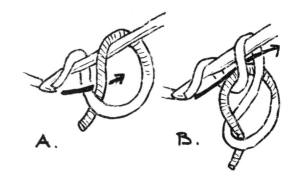

A.   B.

DOUBLE the stitches by
working Yarn Over, Knit
1 around. (18 stitches)

KNIT 3 ROUNDS.

DOUBLE AGAIN (same
way) to 36 stitches,

KNIT 6 ROUNDS.

DOUBLE again to 72
stitches.

C.

KNIT 12 ROUNDS, and
so on.

By the time you have 576 stitches, your shawl will be
about big enough. You may incorporate as many stitch-
patterns as you please between the increase-rounds.

FOR THE BORDER: pick a pretty lace pattern out of
Barbara Abbey, Barbara Walker or wherever, (see appendix)
--and DO NOT CAST OFF. Casting off has a terrible effect
on shawls.

INSTEAD, CAST ON enough stitches for the lace-border,
and KNIT it on to the edge of the shawl, having the lacy
edge outside and the straight edge towards the shawl.

FIGURE 85 - THE PI SHAWL.

AT THE END of every second row, you will knit the last (straight-edge) stitch together with one of the stitches from the edge of the shawl -- AND THUS NIBBLE away at the un-cast-off stitches until you have travelled around the whole periphery.

YOU MAY ALSO crochet an edge (see figure 83) by joining the stitches in groups of 6-or-so, and having a longer or shorter piece of chain between them.

WHEN BLOCKING the crocheted edge, pin out the loops to form a pointed, lacy edge.

THE ORIGINAL SHETLAND SHAWL

MADE without any casting-on or casting-off, the ORIGINAL SHETLAND SHAWL does contain a few adroit tricks.

START by working the lace-border for one side.

KNIT UP along its straight edge and WORK one of the sides in pattern, narrowing this at its edges. (see figure 86)

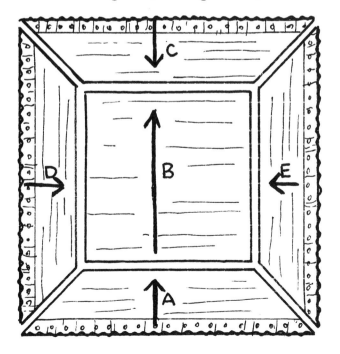

FIGURE 86 – TRADITIONAL SHETLAND SHAWL. C, D, and E are grafted (woven) to center square B.

WHEN IT IS long enough, WORK a row of
misleading holes (Yarn Over, K 2 Together).

NOW, on these stitches, WORK the
center square, and leave it on a piece of wool.

START the opposite side as above and
WEAVE IT to the center-square.

REPEAT for the other two sides, and
WEAVE the four diagonals together.

NOW, I put it to you that this shawl, although never
cast on or off, contains quite a bit of JOINING.

TRY THIS ONE :

THE STONINGTON SHETLAND SHAWL

For the STONINGTON SHETLAND SHAWL, Knit
the center square diagonally (see figure 87),
by starting with 2 stitches and INCREASING 1
stitch at the beginning of each row of garter-
stitch until it is wide enough. (Mine is
approximately 26 inches.)

THEN DECREASE 1 stitch at the beginning of
each row, down to 1 stitch. DO NOT
BREAK WOOL.

KNIT UP along one side of the square at
the rate of 3 stitches for every 2 ridges.

NOW, work on these stitches (in pattern
if you like), for 12-15 inches; INCREASING
1 stitch at the beginning of each row.
DoNotBreakWool, and do not cast off.

*LEAVING the stitches on the needle (or on
a piece of wool), KNIT UP 1 stitch for each
ridge along the side of the trapezoid just
knitted, and 3 stitches for 2 ridges along the
next side of the square.

INCREASE 1 stitch on the open side at the

beginning of every row -- and on the picked-up side, of course, KNIT ON one more picked-up stitch. D.N.B.W.

REPEAT FROM * TWICE MORE. On the FOURTH trapezoid you will knit on a picked-up stitch from either side. D.N.B.W. (The millions of stitches may be a bit crowded on the needle, but will be diminishing from now on.)

CAST ON enough stitches for a lace border

STONINGTON SHAWL

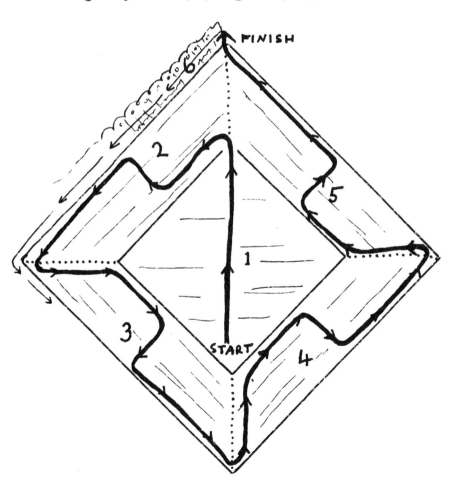

FIGURE 88 - Close-up of the STONINGTON SHAWL showing one corner of the sideways lace border.

and work back and forth on it (see figure 88), WORKING the last stitch of every 2nd row together with one stitch of the shawl.

BEFORE YOU KNOW IT, you're at the first corner. WORK a few extra rows of lace-pattern here, if you wish, to make it go around the corner more easily.

REPEAT for the remaining three sides.

BREAK WOOL and WEAVE the ends of the lace border.

FIGURE 89 -
THE SPOKE SHAWL
(opposite)

THE SPOKE SHAWL , shown in Icelandic Wool, is
DOUBLE INCREASED (by YO, K 1, YO) at 7 points every
4th round -- for straight spokes -- and you can put any patterns or lace-motifs you wish between the spokes. (see
figure 89)

MAKE it in single-ply Icelandic Wool, which is surprisingly strong and WARM when knitted.

CAST ON 7 stitches as Emily Ocker would,
(see figure 84) and DOUBLE INCREASE
every 4th round.

THERE WILL SOON be room for patterns
between the spokes.

WHEN your circle is large enough, CAST
ON and work the lace-or garter-stitch-
border around -- as in the Stonington Shawl.

TO SPIRAL the spokes to the RIGHT -- use
a single INCREASE at 7 points every 2nd
round: Yarn Over, K 2 together, Yarn Over.
TO SPIRAL the spokes to the LEFT : YO, SSK, YO every
2nd round.

THE INNER DIRECTED SHAWL

is spiraled to the LEFT as described above. The totally random pattern is achieved by eratic Yarn-Overs, but each one compensated for by a DE-CREASE of one stitch at the same time, so that you don't lose count. (see figure 90)

FIGURE 90 - THE INNER-DIRECTED SHAWL spirals to the left, and is finished off with a sideways garter-stitch border. #10½ needles were used.

SOMETIMES a GIANT YARN OVER is made by WRAPPING the wool 2-or-3 times around the needle, but this must be treated as one stitch on the next round.

THE BABY SHAWL

Worked in Shetland Jumper-weight, the BABY SHAWL from <u>Knitter's Almanac</u> is square: (see figure 91)

MADE SO by starting with Emily Ocker's beginning and 8 stitches.

IT IS more convenient to work it on 4 double-pointed needles (knitting with a 5th) to start with, so that each quarter has a needle to itself. You can keep track of the increases more easily this way.

These are DOUBLE-IN-CREASES, one each side of each corner-stitch every second round.

If you IN-CREASE by the backward-loop (Make 1) it will be neat and unobtrusive.

If you use YARN OVER (which is only Make 1 without the twist) it will be open and lacy.

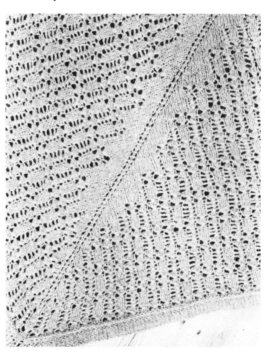

FIGURE 91 - Close-up of the SHETLAND BABY SHAWL.

By the time you have INCREASED to 50 stitches, you can change to a 16 inch circular needle, and soon after, to a 24 inch one.

I've never found it necessary to use a needle longer than 24 inch.

GOOD BOOKS FOR LACE-PATTERN STITCHES:

KNITTING LACE by Barbara Abbey

A TREASURY OF KNITTING PATTERNS and
A SECOND TREASURY OF KNITTING PATTERNS
by Barbara Walker

FIRST BOOK OF MODERN LACE KNITTING and
SECOND BOOK OF MODERN LACE KNITTING
by Marianne Kinzel

THE ART OF SHETLAND LACE
by Sarah Don

(see Bibliography)

FAIR ISLE SWEATERS

Clockwise from center front; Stu's vest (see appendix),
Liesl's pullover, Gaffer's vest, and Cully's vest.

LESSON FOUR

ARANS, GUERNSEYS AND FAIR ISLES

There are three kinds of traditional jerseys which have their roots in the British Isles. The names JERSEY and GUERNSEY (or GANSEY) are interchangeable, and are derived from the names of the Channel Islands: Jersey, Guernsey, Alderney, and Sark -- where a handknitting cottage industry for these almost indestructible garments flourished in the 19th century.

They are all beautiful, and NOT SIMPLE to knit, but FAR SIMPLER than they appear to be if you keep your head, and make your own decisions.

There is NO RULE that you can't do what you like with a given pattern or shape, and this APPLIES TO ALL KNITTING DIRECTIONS.

WHEN you find some detail about which you have the slightest doubt, or think might be improved, then DOUBT IT and, possibly, IMPROVE IT.

DO WHAT YOU LIKE with knitting directions (including tossing them out the window) -- they are just there for a guide.

FIGURE 92 - My first Aran, made on two needles before I knew any better. After many years of wear, the cuffs went, but the elbows were saved by Heart Patches. (see appendix)

FOR EXAMPLE:

IN THIS ARAN sweater (see figure 92) there is a series of diamonds filled with reverse stocking-stitch.

BY THE TIME I approached the second diamond, I realized there were more possibilities than this, and filled it with stocking-stitch -- thinking that alternate diamonds would be nice.

AT THE THIRD diamond, I thought WHY NOT have all the diamonds filled differently ?

THUS COMMITTED, I filled them with seed-stitch; K 1, P 1 rib; garter-stitch; that strange heel-stitch where alternate stitches are slipped on alternate rows; and finally, double seed-stitch.

THIS ABOUT EXHAUSTED my fillings as well as the necessary length for the sweater. But STUDY Barbara Walker's TREASURY OF KNITTING PATTERNS and you will find scores more of simple texture-variations.

THE FISHTRAP ARAN

In the FISHTRAP ARAN I took just the main pattern from Gladys Thompson's PATTERNS FOR GUERNSEYS, JERSEYS, AND ARANS. It has no name, so we christened it Fishtrap, which we consider descriptive and appropriate.

The construction is identical to that of the drop-shoulder ski-sweater. (see figure 93)

FIGURE 93 - THE FISHTRAP ARAN; basic drop-shoulder construction, knitted in 2-ply oatmeal Sheepswool.

THE HAND-TO-HAND ARAN I "unvented". (see figure 94) It is pleasant to knit; you work on the cabled sleeves-cum-yoke when you are full of prance, and the plain body when you are at a meeting.

USE ANY cables or patterns that please you.

FIGURE 94 - THE HAND-TO-HAND ARAN, in 3-ply oatmeal Sheepswool. Heavily textured sleeves and yoke knitted from cuff-to-cuff, and plain body.

THE SLEEVES, of course, are worked on a 16 inch
circular needle, but for the yoke you must
divide and work back-and-forth; necessary to
the design construction. (see appendix)

I DID NOT unvent the making of ARANS on circular
needles. Gladys Thompson told me that she did this too, but
that her publishers were afraid of making knitters afraid,
and excised this fact. Can you IMAGINE?

The original Irish knitters surely made them round and
round, but of course on four -- or even more -- needles.
The lovely Aran jerseys have been knitted on the Isles of
Aran off the Irish coast for many generations, but came to
light in this country in 1955.

Gladys Thompson added them almost as an afterthought
to her book of British Fisherman's Jerseys, and the pertinent
section of this fine book has become the Aran-knitter's
bible. Now the first, and larger, section is coming into its
own.

GUERNSEYS

The typical navy-blue or black jersey of the commercial fishermen was very tightly knitted in strong wool, and was extremely wind-and-weatherproof. Oilskin trousers were worn over them which did not, of course, cover the shoulders -- so the latter were executed with as many elaborate patterns as possible to thicken them and make them warmer.

The sleeves were rather short to save them from wetness when the lines were dragged in, and were provided with comfortable, seamless gussets -- knitted in one with the body. Sleeves were then knitted up at the armholes and worked downwards.

It has occured to us that if the knitters of yore had been provided with our natural, oatmeal-colored, unbleached (water-repellent) wool, they would have used this for their jerseys. SO we frequently make our jerseys with this wool, as shown in figure 96, and very nice they look, too.

FIGURE 95 - (opposite). A 4-ply cream Aran cardigan. Patterns from left; Cross-Banded Cable*, Sheepfold[2], Ribbed Cable[3], and at mid-back, Double X Cable*.
* B. Walker - CHARTED
[2] E. Zimmermann - Newsletter #6
[3] B. Walker - TREASURY

FIGURE 96 - GAFFER'S GANSEY is shown being modeled by HIMSELF on the dedication page. Note the continuous side-seam/ gusset. (see appendix)

ANOTHER good idea is to use a grey-blue wool -- the color of the navy blue jersey after years of sun and salt-water have been at it.

SOME of the patterns are very elaborate indeed, (see Mrs. Laidlaw's Pattern in figure 97) even though they are worked in Knit and Purl only. Cables are also frequently used.

Even the simple patterns need careful attention and a good light to work by. Somewhere I read that these dark ganseys were only knitted by daylight.

FIGURE 97 - MRS. LAIDLAW'S PATTERN adapted by Meg to a 5 to the inch GAUGE. It is reversible because of the garter-stitch strips at the armholes and looks good either way out. (see Part II, Lesson 4.)

GANSEY PATTERNS were native to the villages of the British Isles almost as Tartans were (and still are) to the Scottish clans.

The pattern in figure 96 was taken from p. 66 of the book CORNISH GUERNSEYS AND KNIT FROCKS. I have adapted it slightly from the authentic method of construction by means of short rows across the back, cut armholes, and the neck and shoulder treatment. The latter is described in detail in the appendix.

THESE CHANGES didn't alter the shape of the sweater; I put myself into the frame of mind of a Cornish knitter with no printed instructions, but WITH a circular needle.

*   *   *   *   *

FAIR ISLES

AT LAST we come to the jerseys of Scotland, the Shetland Islands, and Fair Isle. They appear more difficult than the plain-blue gansey sweaters; but are really easier, as you will be dealing with easily distinguishable colors, instead of almost INdistinguishable knit and purl in a dark color.

THEY MUST be made of SHETLAND WOOL if you want the Real Thing, and this brings me to an admonition to study so-called "shetland wool" very closely.

BY LAW, the company must state on the package the actual content of the yarn, as well as the exact percentage of Shetland Wool it contains.

SHETLAND WOOL is like port: if it's called "PORT" it must come from Portugal; if it comes from somewhere

else it must be modified by its area of provenance --
California Port, or Wisconsin Port or whatever.

BE ON YOUR GUARD for Truth in Advertising and
DESPISE FEINTS AND BLATHER.

In Germany I was told that the word <u>Wolle</u> (German
for wool) is now recognized as a generic term for <u>Garn</u>
(yarn) and that Wolle may contain any revolting fiber that
the manufacturer wishes to incorporate.

SO KEEP YOUR EYES OPEN and your brain humming.

FAIR ISLES, then, are knitted in patterns and colors of
the most perfect and restrained designs. The material is
wool blended from natural sheep colors, sometimes dyed to
other muted shades, and pointed up by pure blacksheep and
pure whitesheep, which are NOT QUITE black or white, but more beautiful.

FIGURE - 99 Close-up of LIESL'S
FAIR ISLE. The dark is natural
black, the light is honey-beige,
and the background, Ghillie green.

THE DESIGNS employed are typical, and usually consist of alternate diagonal crosses and diamond shapes, both of which are quite shallow and wide -- sometimes taking up to 30 stitches for one pattern-repeat, but often more like 20 or 22.

AS YOU CAN SEE, considerable thought is needed to fit these into a sweater of a certain size.

There are also many beautiful smaller patterns, and, recently I believe, a great infiltration of the heart motif, which shows the influence that one tradition may receive from others.

BE ALL THIS AS IT MAY, -- and I would urge that you use ANY designs and colors that appeal to you within the discipline of this particular art -- I have yet to describe the most typical aspect of FAIR ISLE KNITTING, which I have not observed elsewhere:

> A FAIR ISLE pattern will blend
> the color of a pattern through
> several colors WITHIN THE CON-
> FINES OF A SINGLE PATTERN-
> REPEAT.

THUS, for instance, the motif itself may go through two rounds of blacksheep, two rounds of Moorit (a gentle brown), and one round of a muted yellow, -- and back through two rounds of Moorit to two rounds of blacksheep. (study figures 99 and 100)

AT THE SAME TIME the background color may vary from beige, through pale green, to deep green and back again.

YOU WILL SEE that there are infinite possibil- ities of variation, even if you repeat the same pattern throughout the garment.

OR, you may maintain the pattern-shadings and vary the patterns.

BY SKILLFUL manipula- tion of the principles of vary- ing the patterns and varying the arrangements of colors within the patterns, you can give the impression of having absolutely no pattern-repeats within a single garment, or even within a series of garments.

FIGURE 100 - CULLY'S FAIR ISLE, in close-up, alternates bands of blues, browns, and greens on a natural black background.

To quote the old Gertie Lawrence song: "Experiment -- and you'll see. "

EXPERIMENT WITH TAMS

FIGURE 102 TAM-O'-SHANTER:

A. COMPLETED.

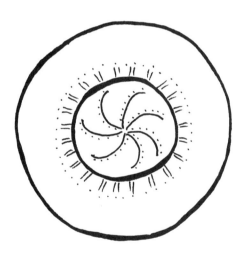

B. STRETCH OVER 10" CARDBOARD

A TAM-O-SHANTER is rather like that hat you made in Part 1, but on more stitches at a smaller GAUGE, with a greater INCREASE, and blocked over a dinner plate.

FIGURE 103 - Stu's FAIR ISLE VEST. For complete instructions, see appendix.

FAIR ISLES are simply shaped, hewing to the ski-sweater line. They do vary by frequently incorporating the V-Neck, which is knitted in one with the circular shaping:

AFTER ARMHOLE SHAPING (see below), put two stitches at center-front on a safety-pin, and CAST ON 3 or 4 stitches instead.

THE 2 STITCHES will form the center-stitches of the future neck-ribbing, and the 3 or 4 stitches will serve for the future CUTTING for the neck.

IT LOOKS GOOD to decrease the neck at the rate of ONE STITCH EACH SIDE every SECOND ROUND until the wanted amount of stitches (very often about 6 inches worth) have been DECREASED.

THEN WORK STRAIGHT to wanted length. This gives a slight curve to the neckline which fits well and looks good.

ARMHOLES have been shaped in a similar fashion, with more stitches on a thread to start with, and fewer decreases -- and are then worked, of course, straight to shoulder.

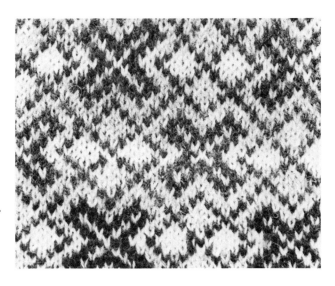

FIGURE 104 -
In Gaffer's
sweater you can
see rows of
white so cun-
ningly employed
that you would
swear that three
colors have been
used at once.
But they haven't.

We realize that the knitted projects in this Third
Part have been sometimes rather sketchily described, but
you are, after all, now Master-Knitters, and no Master-
Knitter would consider even existing without his or her
comforting bookshelf of mixed books on knitting.

AND WHEN I SAY BOOKS, I mean serious treatises on
techniques, patterns, and traditions. We have compiled
a list of such books in the Bibliography section to follow.

CLOSING STATEMENT

I have been encouraged to end this book with a closing
statement. (After all, where else could it be?)

REALLY, the whole book is an OPENING STATEMENT.
It attempts to introduce you to a few -- perhaps many --
knitting techniques which may change your knitting-habits.
Please consider them by trying them out.

Knitting has been a comfort and an inspiration to people
for hundreds -- perhaps thousands -- of years, and during
this time methods have been discovered, forgotten, distorted,
improved upon, forgotten again, and re-discovered to be
improved upon yet again.

It would be pompous indeed to imagine that any strange,
new technique is really NEW. But we shall never know. A
recent invention is the wooden circular needle. This material
is god-given for the making of the first circular needle on
Earth, and who is to say that it is not a re-invention?

KEEP DIGGING, you archaeologists, you may yet find one
in a tomb, in a bog, or in some lost and forgotten knitting-
bag.

Maintain an open mind, then, and perhaps develop for
yourself a new way of life and. . . .

Good Knitting—

Elizabeth.

SCHOOLHOUSE PRESS
6899 CARY BLUFF
PITTSVILLE, WI. 54466

BIBLIOGRAPHY

ABBEY, Barbara. KNITTING LACE. Viking.
New York, 1974

DALE YARN CO. KNIT YOUR OWN NORWEGIAN
SWEATER. Dover. New York, 1974

DEBES, Hans. FØROYSK BINDINGARMYNSTER
Gotu. Faroe Islands, 1969

DON, Sarah. FAIR ISLE KNITTING. Bell & Hyman.
London, 1978

DON, Sarah. THE ART OF SHETLAND LACE.
Bell & Hyman. London, 1980

GAINFORD, Veronica. DESIGNS FOR KNITTING KILT
HOSE AND KNICKERBOCKER STOCKINGS.
Rannoch Press. Glasgow, 1980

HARVEY, Michael. FISHERMAN KNITTING.
Shire. London, 1980

KINZEL, Marianne. THE FIRST BOOK OF MODERN
LACE KNITTING. Dover. New York, 1972

KINZEL, Marianne. THE SECOND BOOK OF MODERN
LACE KNITTING. Dover. New York, 1972

SIBBERN-BØHN. NORWEGIAN KNITTING DESIGNS
Grøndahl & Søn. Oslo, 1965

THOMAS, Mary. MARY THOMAS'S KNITTING BOOK
Dover. New York, 1972

THOMAS, Mary. MARY THOMAS'S BOOK OF KNITTING
PATTERNS. Dover. New York, 1972

THOMPSON, Gladys. PATTERNS FOR GUERNSEYS, JERSEYS & ARANS. Dover. New York, 1979

WALKER, Barbara. A TREASURY OF KNITTING PATTERNS. Scribners. New York, 1968

WALKER, Barbara. A SECOND TREASURY OF KNITTING PATTERNS. Scribners. New York, 1970

WRIGHT, Mary. CORNISH GUERNSEYS & KNIT-FROCKS. Hodge. Cornwall, 1979

ZIMMERMANN, Elizabeth. KNITTING WITHOUT TEARS. Scribners. New York, 1971

ZIMMERMANN, Elizabeth. KNITTER'S ALMANAC. Scribners. New York, 1974

Elizabeth Zimmermann's
NEWSLETTERS - 1958 to 1969

1. Shetland Fair Isle yoke sweater *
2. Scandinavian ski-sweater *
3. 36 graphs for color-pattern knitting
4. Saddle-shoulder Brooks sweater *
5. Heavy ribbed sweater and cap
6. Aran sweater or cardigan *
7. Child's hooded jacket; garter-stitch
8. Raglan sweater or cardigan *
9. Blanket or afghan; garter-stitch
10. Heavy woodsman's socks. 4 d.p. needles
11. 5 caps for a 16" circular needle *
12. V-necked, drop-shouldered Aran *
13. Graph for the " 1 & 3 " sweater
14. Icelandic yoke sweater *
15. 4-needle mittens
16. 8 knitting tips for circular needles
17. Tights for children and adults *
18. Ski-stockings for 4 needles
19. Spiral Sheepsdown hat *
20. Kangaroo-pouch sweater *
21. Babies' garter-stitch Surprise Jacket
22. Bonnet, booties and bunting in garter-stitch

* means for circular needles
(Editor's note to sixth printing: Newsletters are now
o.o.p., but nearly every design is available in
Elizabeth's other books.)

SPIN-OFFS

1. Adult Surprise Jacket
2. New Zealand Sweater*
3. Fair Isle Yoke Sweater*

Elizabeth Zimmermann's
<u>WOOL GATHERINGS</u> - 1969 to 1981

1. Pi shawl *
2. Sweaters from the neck down *
3. Heavy garter-stitch jacket
4. Ponchos *
5. Lap-shoulder sweater *
6. A mittful of mittens
7. Aspen yoke sweater * and Rib Warmer
8. Six woolly hats *
9. Long, collared garter-stitch jacket
10. Vests and Tops. Three of them *
11. Child's Fair Isle Yoke sweater. Four sizes *
12. V-neck sweater; set-in sleeves *
13. Shaded Aspen or Diamond ski sweater *
14. Hand-to-Hand sweater; Aran * or garter-stitch
15. Stonington Shetland shawl
16. Pelerine *
17. Afghan/Sweater and slippers. Garter-stitch
18. Nalgar (backwards raglan) *
19. Rorschach sweater in garter-stitch
20. Five more woolly hats
21. Suspender sweater. Garter-stitch
22. Vests and Tops again *
23. Garter-stitch Epaulet Jacket
24. Fair Isle jerseys; sweaters & vests *
25. Fisherman's Guernseys *
26. Swedish <u>Bohus</u> Sweater *
27. The Bog <u>Shirt</u>. Garter-stitch
28. The Moebius. Garter-stitch
29. Three Bavarian Sweaters
30. Square-rigged Vests *
31. Box-The-Compass Yoke *
32. Basket-weave Sweater & Tam *
33. Circle Yoke * & Tam
34. 3-Cornered Shawls
35. 2-End Knitting *

WOOL GATHERING is a twice yearly (fall & spring) knitting publication by Elizabeth Zimmermann and Meg Swansen. It contains new patterns in each issue plus information about new books, wools, and related knitter's needs. From:

SCHOOLHOUSE PRESS
6899 CARY BLUFF
PITTSVILLE, WI. 54466

APPENDIX

EDITORS' NOTE: Elizabeth wanted us to put a large DO NOT READ sign at the beginning of this appendix to show her hope that by the time knitters have gone through the twelve lessons and experimented with the various techniques contained therein, they will never have to follow stitch-for-stitch directions again.

However, in order to touch all the bases and accomodate those devoted knitters who, like so many of the woolly beasts who started all this, are born followers, we have prevailed upon Elizabeth to allow us to print BLIND FOLLOWERS DIRECTIONS for a number of garments shown and explained in the video lessons and book.

We also hope that those of you who are not BLIND FOLLOWERS may be able to clear up questions about some fine-point or trouble-spot corner you may knit yourself into as you fly from the nest of rigid directions. Check these directions and see how Elizabeth did it - stitch for stitch - and then "unvent" something like it to solve your own problem. It's all knitting, and you're in charge.

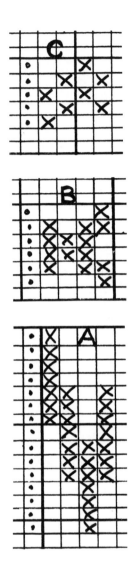

FIGURE 106

ICELANDIC YOKE SWEATER

GAUGE: 4 stitches to 1". Get it right.
SIZES: 38" (40") around
MATERIALS: 24oz Icelandic wool for body
(worked doubled); 4oz for yoke pattern.
24" and 16" circular needles of a size to give
you the above GAUGE (approx. #7, 8 or 9);
1 set d.p. needles of the same size.

BODY: With 24" needle, cast on 152 (160) stitches.
JOIN, being careful not to twist. KNIT for 17" -
or desired length to underarm.
PUT 12 stitches (approx. 8% of body stitches)
on pieces of wool at each underarm. Set body
aside and begin
SLEEVE: Cast on 30 (32) stitches (20% of body
stitches) on d.p. needles. JOIN.
WORK in knit, increasing 2 stitches at underarm
every 5th round. Change to 16" needle when
practicable.
AT 50 (54) stitches (33% of body stitches),
work straight to 18", or desired length to underarm.
PUT 12 stitches on a piece of wool. Make another
sleeve and
PUT ALL STITCHES of body and sleeves (minus
the 8% at underarms) on 24" needle; matching
underarms. (see page 40).
YOKE : Knit 1½", then work PATTERN A,
changing pattern rounds behind left shoulder for
pullover - or at center-front if you plan to cut
later for a cardigan.
WORK DECREASE rounds as follows:
K 1, K 2 together around.
Work PATTERN B. Repeat decrease round.
Work PATTERN C. Repeat decrease round.
You should now have approx. 40% of body stitches.
FOR VITAL Back-of-neck-shaping, see pages 47
& 48.
FOR A CARDIGAN see pages 72 & 73.

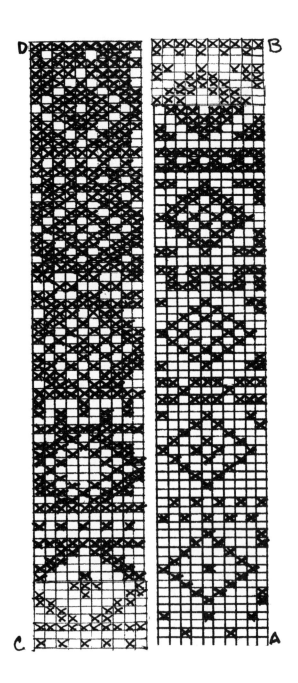

FIGURE 107 –
DIAMOND GRAPH.
Work from right to
left. Start at A,
work to B, then to
C, then to D. This
graph is inter-
changeable with the
ASPEN GRAPH on page
59.

SHADED ASPEN-LEAF SWEATER

GAUGE: 4½ stitches to 1". Get it right.
SIZES: 37" (40", 42½", 45") chest measurement.
MATERIALS: 2-ply Sheepswool, or "Homespun"
or Fisherman wool: 6 (6, 7, 7) 4oz skeins of the
background color, 3 (3, 3, 4) skeins pattern color.
1 16", 1 24" circular needle of a size to give you
the above GAUGE.

CAST ON on 24" needle 168 (180, 192, 204)
stitches for body. Join, being careful not to twist,
and knit around for 3 rounds in background color.
Begin pattern on opposite page, always changing
rounds at the same spot; mark the first stitch with
a safety pin. Work for about 27" or to desired
length for completed sweater.
CAST OFF fairly firmly.

SLEEVES: On a 16" needle, loosely cast on 34
(36, 38, 40) stitches. Join, and work around for
3 rounds. Start pattern, centering it, and leaving
the odd stitches for the underarm. Mark the
underarm stitch, and on the 4th round, (and every
succeeding 4th round), INCREASE 1 stitch each
side of marked stitch, by means of M(ake) 1.
AT ABOUT 17" (17", 18", 18") or wanted length
for a drop-shoulder sleeve, cast off fairly loosely.
MAKE another sleeve.

MEASURE for straight armholes the exact length
of the top of the sleeve. RUN a basting-thread
down this line and another across the bottom. With
small machine-stitch, stitch twice each side of
basting and across bottom. CUT between machine-
stitching.

FINISH AS FOR DROP-SHOULDER SWEATER -
pages 65 - 70.

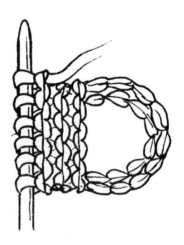

FIGURE 108 - I-CORD
TAB BUTTONHOLE ready
to be woven on to a
garter-stitch border.

RORSCHACH SWEATER

GAUGE: 4 stitches to 1". Get it right.
MATERIALS: 8 (8, 9, 10) 4 oz. skeins of wool
to give this exact GAUGE. 1 pair, or 1 24"
circular needle of a size to give you this GAUGE;
#7 for loose, #10 for tight knitters. Experiment
SIZES: 36" (38", 40", 42") body-width
   23" (24", 25", 26") body-length.

DOUBLE-DECREASE = slip 2 as if to knit, Knit 1,
Pass 2 slipped stitches over. (see page 30).
DOUBLE-INCREASE = Make 1 by backward loop
over right-hand needle. (see page 16).

LEFT SIDE, BACK AND FRONT COMBINED:
CAST ON 198 (206, 214, 222) stitches and work
preparatory row, starting at center-back F:
Knit 92 (96, 100, 104) stitches. Put marker in next
stitch (E), Knit 10, marker in next stitch (D),
Knit 10, marker in next stitch (C), Knit 10,
marker in next stitch (B), Knit 72 (76, 80, 84)
to lower center-front at A.

ROW 1: K 2 together, K to within 1 stitch of B,
double-decrease, K 9 to C, double-increase, K 10
to D, double-increase, K 9 to within 1 stitch of E,
double-decrease, K to end at F.
ROW 2: K 2 together, K to end.
Repeat these 2 rows, putting in stripes as wished.
At 5 ridges increase 10 stitches evenly-spaced
between A and B on front. At a total of 12
(14, 16, 18) ridges, stop decreasing at ends.
NOW "fill in" front below B-C as follows: -

STARTING AT A, * K to B, K 2 together, turn,
K back.
REPEAT from * until C has been decreased away.
Work across to F and repeat, to "fill in" back.

WORK ON ALL STITCHES for a total of 36
(38, 40, 42) ridges OR $\frac{1}{4}$ of wanted body-width.
Put 1/3 of all stitches at each end on threads.
Continue on center 1/3 for:

SLEEVE: Decrease 1 stitch at beginning of each
row for <u>GUSSET</u>. At 50 (52, 54, 56) stitches work
straight to wanted length - about 13" (14", 15", 16").
For a snug cuff K 2 together across at 5" shy of
wanted length; for short snug cuff $2\frac{1}{2}$". Cast off.

WEAVE side-seam (see page 51). Sew sleeve seam.

<u>LOWER SIDE</u>: K up 1 stitch for each ridge from
A - F, and knit to fill in lower space. K up 1
stitch from diagonals at end of each row, matching
stripes, if any. 5 ridges before end, decrease 6
stitches evenly-spaced across. Cast off.

<u>RIGHT SIDE, BACK AND FRONT COMBINED</u> is a
mirror-image of left side. On preparatory row,
K 72 (76, 80, 84), repeat center-section, and end
with K 92 (96, 100, 104) stitches. Sew halves at
center-back. K 16 (18, 20, 22) ridges tightly on
6 stitches in finer wool and sew in at neck-back
to prevent lateral stretch.

<u>BELT</u>: Cast on 140 (150, 160, 170) stitches and
K 6 ridges. Cast off fairly loosley.

<u>BELT LOOPS</u>: On 12 stitches K 4 ridges. Cast
off and sew at underarm waistline.

Editors' note   for the second printing:

<u>EPS</u>   or

<u>E</u>lizabeth's <u>P</u>ercentage <u>S</u>ystem.

    Knitters keep telling us that Elizabeth's
percentage method of designing one's own sweater
is NEW and WELCOME to them. Elizabeth "unvented"
the basic concept 25 years ago and has been refining
it ever since; but it wasn't until <u>Wool Gathering #26</u>
that we came up with the above title of EPS. It boils
down to the fact that in a nicely-proportioned garment,
a certain series of measurements will always have the
same relationship, one to another.

    This method is governed by its KEY-NUMBER [K] ,
which is the number of stitches around the BODY.
SLEEVES start with 20% of [K] , and are increased at
the rate of 2 stitches every 5th round at the underarm
"seam" to 33% of [K] for a yoke sweater. (for drop-
shoulder EPS, see below) They are then worked straight
to the wanted length to underarm - about 18" for most
adults. 8% of [K] is placed on pieces of wool at the
exact underarms of sleeves and body, and all remaining
stitches are put on a 24" circular needle with underarms matching. The YOKE DEPTH is 1/4 [K] - expressed
in inches, not stitches. Adult yokes are shaped by three
33% decrease-rounds (K1, K2 tog). Where you place them
- more or less equally spaced - is up to you and to the
incidence of patterns; but DON'T start them until the
yoke is about HALF-knitted. The remaining neck stitches will be 40% [K[, more or less.

    Small CHILDREN'S yokes have their own idiosyn-
cratic shaping: 1/3, 1/3, <u>1/4</u> (you may place the 1/4
decrease in any of the three spots), which results

in a 50% [K] neck opening, as children have relatively larger heads than adults.

DROP-SHOULDER sleeves are increased 2 stitches every 4th round to 50% of [K]. The drop-shoulder body is worked straight to desired length and the middle 1/3 of the top is the neck opening.

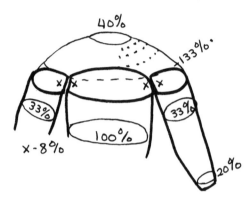

YOKE EPS

BODY----------------------100% = KEY NUMBER [K]
WRIST ----------------------20% of [K]
UPPER ARM -------------33% of [K]
UNDERARM -------------- 8% of [K]
Circumference of Shoulders -- 133% of [K]
NECK --------------------- 40% of [K]

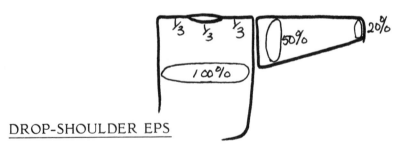

DROP-SHOULDER EPS

BODY -------------------- 100% = KEY NUMBER [K]
WRIST -------------------- 20% of [K]
UPPER ARM ------------- 50% of [K]
NECK -------------------- 33% of [K]

HEART HAT (OR ELBOW PATCH)

GAUGE: 4 stitches to 1"
SIZE: adult
MATERIALS: 3-4 ounces of wool. 16" circular needle (work in garter-stitch back-and-forth) of a size to give you the above GAUGE.

CAST ON 61 stitches. After the first row, SLIP ALL FIRST STITCHES.

Row 1: K29, sl 1, K2tog, psso, K26, K2tog, TURN.
   Row 2: K54, K2tog, TURN.
Row 3: K26, sl 1, K2tog, psso, K23, K2tog, TURN.
   Row 4. K48, K2tog, TURN.
Row 5: K23, sl 1, K2tog, psso, K20, K2tog, TURN.
   Row 6: K42, K2tog, TURN.
Row 7: K20, sl 1, K2tog, psso, K17, K2tog, TURN.
   Row 8: K36, K2tog, TURN.
Row 9: K17, sl 1, K2tog, psso, K14, K2tog, TURN.
   Row 10: K30, K2tog, TURN.
Row 11: K14, sl 1, K2tog, psso, K11, K2tog, TURN.
   Row 12: K24, K2tog, TURN.
Row 13: K11, sl 1, K2tog, psso, K10, K2tog, TURN.
   Row 14: K22, K2tog, TURN.
Row 15: K10, sl 1, K2tog, psso, K9, K2tog, TURN.
   Row 16: K20, K2tog, TURN.
Row 17: K9, sl 1, K2tog, psso, K8, K2tog, TURN.
   Row 18: K18, K2tog, TURN.
Row 19: K8, sl 1, K2tog, psso, K7, K2tog, TURN.
   Row 20: K16, K2tog, TURN.
Row 21: K7, sl 1, K2tog, psso, K6, K2tog, TURN.
   Row 22: K14, K2tog, TURN.
Row 23: K6, sl 1, K2tog, psso, K5, K2tog, TURN.
   Row 24: K12, K2tog, FINISH.

13 STITCHES should remain (20% of 61 + 1).
Break wool. (For elbow-patch cast off tightly.)

NOW TURN THE HEART INTO A HAT :

Starting at the POINT (prehaps in a different
color), knit up all stitches along the edge.
Here is where the 16" circular needle is
unbeatable.
KNIT back & forth for $4\frac{1}{2}$". Now K8, K2 tog
across (10% decrease), and knit for 1" more,
or to desired depth Cast off in I-Cord (p 106)
I-CORD TIE: work I-Cord as on page 105 for
about 15". Then -
PICK UP all stitches along lower edge of bonnet
and work I-CORD CASTING OFF (see page 106),
finishing with another 15" of I-Cord tie. Done.

MAKE HEARTS in any size you wish by using a
multiple of 10 stitches + 1.
THE NUMBER of orphan stitches gradually
deserted at the ends will be 10% + 1 of the
number of cast-on stitches; and the final un-cast-
off stitches will be 20% + 1.
WHEN KNITTING UP STITCHES around heart,
perform this from the "wrong" side. If you have
cast on by the long-tail method, the fabric will
blend undetectably.

BABIES' GARTER-STITCH SURPRISE JACKET

MATERIALS: 3oz Shetland Wool, a 24" circular needle
(work back and forth for garter-stitch) of a size to
give you a GAUGE of 6 sts to 1", and 5 little buttons.

Make a SWATCH to determine your GAUGE, and

CAST-ON 160 sts. With safety pins, mark the 36th and
the 125th stitches.

1. K34, sl 1, K2 tog, psso, K86, sl 1, K2 tog, psso, K34.
2. and all even-numbered rows, KNIT.
3. K33, sl 1, K2 tog, psso, K84, sl 1, K2 tog, psso, K33.
5. K32, sl 1, K2 tog, psso, K82, sl 1, K2 tog, psso, K32.
7. K31, sl 1, K2 tog, psso, K80, sl 1, K2 tog, psso, K31.

See what you are doing? You are decreasing 2 at each
marked stitch, making 2 diagonal lines, and 2 corners.
At 5 ridges INCREASE 9 sts (K3, M1) across end sections,
believe it or not for fullness above CUFF. After 22
DECREASES (90 sts), work 3 rows even, then start to
INCREASE at the same points, by M1 each side of marked
stitch every 2nd row. Work will start to look very odd,
indeed, but trust me, and PRESS ON. At 114 sts, increase
10 sts in 1 row evenly-spaced across center section for
BACK FULLNESS.

At 152 sts, SHAPE NECK by casting off 5 sts at beginnings
of next two rows. When there are 158 sts, work on CENTER
90 sts only, for 10 ridges. Hope you are still with me.

NOW pick up 10 sts from side of piece just knitted, K 34 sts
from end of needle. Work next row, repeating this process
(178 sts). Mark 44th and 135th sts, and start increasing
by M1 each side of marked stitch every 2nd row. After 3
ridges, work 5 small buttonholes (Yarn Over, K2 tog) evenly-
spaced on end sections. Work 3 ridges and CAST OFF, fairly
loosely, in PURL, on the right side.

Funny-looking object, isn't it? Well, study the drawing on
page 100; match A to A and B to B, join with a neat woven
seam, and hey presto eureka and lo -- a baby sweater!

When you know if it's a boy or girl, sew buttons over buttonholes
on appropriate side. The baby will probably be UNMOVED by this
offering, but the mother may well be charmed, and your friends
will be AMAZED.

FIGURE 109 ✻

<u>A PIECE OF SHAPING TO ELIMINATE BULKY UNDERARMS:</u>
On front, knit to within 10 (12, 14) stitches of
underarm, turn. Purl to within 10 (12, 14) stitches
of underarm, turn. Knit to within 8 (10, 12) stitches
of underarm, turn. Purl to within 8 (10, 12) stitches
of underarm, turn. Continue thus, 2 more stitches each
row, until you have reached the underarm. Repeat on back.

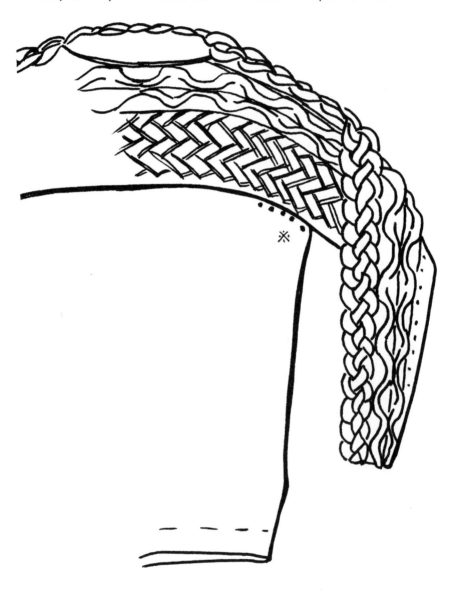

HAND-TO-HAND ARAN PULLOVER

GAUGE: 4 stitches to 1", measured over stocking stitch. Get it right.
SIZES: 38" (40", 42") chest.
MATERIALS: 8 (8, 9) 4 oz skeins 3-ply Sheepswool. 1 24" circular needle of a size to give you the above GAUGE, roughly #7 - #10.
KEY NUMBER of body=stitches: 152 (160, 168).

STARTING AT RIGHTHAND CUFF : CAST ON 46 (48, 50) stitches (which are 25% of the body-stitches plus 7, because the cables "take up". WORK BACK AND FORTH on the circular needle, or on straight needles.
SLIP ALL FIRST STITCHES.

ESTABLISH CABLES: a 4-strand cable is in the middle, flanked by Double O cables. These will be divided by P 1, K 1 back, P 1, and will take up 44 stitches. The end stitches are worked in reverse stocking-stitch; purled on the right side and knitted on the inside, and will be increased by 1 stitch each side of the cables every 4th row.
WHEN YOU HAVE half the number of your key-number of body-stitches (76 ((80. 84))), work straight to neck-opening, 24" (25", 26").

DOUBLE O CABLE: 13 stitches wide, 24 rows high.
ROW 1 (wrong side): * P 6, K 1, P 6.
ROW 2: Take 3 stitches on spare needle and hold in back. K 3, K 3 from spare needle (Left over Right cable), P 1, take 3 stitches on spare needle and hold in front, K 3, K 3 from spare needle, (Right over Left cable).
ROWS 3 through 13: Knit the K stitches and purl the P stitches.
ROW 14: Right over Left cable, P 1, Left over Right cable.
ROWS 15 through 24: Knit the K stitches and purl the P stitches. Repeat from *.

4-STRAND CABLE: 12 stitches wide. 8 rows high.
ROW 1 (wrong side): * P 12.
ROW 2: Right over Left cable twice.
ROWS 3,4,5: P 12 stitches on wrong side; K 12
stitches on right side.
ROW 6: K 3, Left over Right cable, K 3.
ROWS 7 & 8: P 12 stitches on wrong side; K 12
stitches on right side. Repeat from *.

THE CABLES may seem complicated at first, but
you'll soon get the hang of them. The cabling comes
on the same row, so that you have three rows of
peace in between. Don't forget to separate the
three cables by P 1, K 1 B, P 1.
AND DON'T FORGET THE INCREASING: 1 stitch
at each side of the cables every 4th row (on the
cable row if you like) until there are 76 (80, 84)
stitches, about 15" (16", 17") or wanted length
to underarm.
NOW you can introduce a different pattern across
the chest on the 32 (36, 40) stitches you have
increased; 16 (18, 20) on either side. (I used
Barbara Walker's "Fractured Lattice".)

FRACTURED LATTICE: 8 stitches wide. 8 rows high.
LT (Left Twist): Hold 1st stitch in front, K 2nd
stitch, K 1st stitch.
RT (Right Twist): K 2 together, but do not take
off the needle, K 2nd stitch again, take both off
the needle.
ROW 1, and all wrong-side rows: P all stitches.
ROW 2: * LT, K 2, LT, RT, K 2. Repeat from *.
ROW 4: K 1, * LT, K 2, RT, K 2. Repeat from *,
        ending with K 1.
ROW 6: * RT, LT, RT, K 2. Repeat from *.
ROW 8: K 3, * LT, K 2, RT, K 2. Repeat from *,
        ending with LT, K 3.

Now you have three patterns going simultaneously.
Continue without shaping until the piece is long
enough to reach to the beginning of the neck-
opening - about 24" (25", 26). Neck-width will
be about 9", or very roughly half the width of the
body. In order to give it superior shaping, make the
yoke-back longer than the yoke-front by including
the center 4-strand cable with the back. Leave,
therefore, the front 31 (33, 35) stitches on a
piece of wool and continue on the back 45 (47, 49)
stitches.
YES, you will be shy the K 1 B stitch on either
front or back. Just increase an extra stitch on the
back edge.
WHEN you have worked about 9", try the piece on,
in the interest of centering the Double O cable,
if possible. Break the wool, and with it continue
the yoke-front to match.
JOIN both pieces, and continue down the left
sleeve, not forgetting the decreases when the time
comes. When both sleeves match, cast off in pattern.

NOW COMES THE PLAIN PART: Measure off
19" (20", 21") at center-front, and knit up, with
right side towards you, 76 (80. 84) stitches along
this piece. I do this by knitting up 1 stitch in
each of the 3 yoke-stitches, and 2 in the 4th yoke-
stitch, and so on, which rectifies the imbalance
between stitch-count and row-count in stocking-
stitch. If you have not been slipping all first
stitches, you are on your own. ✳ (see page 158)
JOIN, AND WORK AROUND to wanted length,
17" (18", 19"). Put in 3 sets of short rows across
the back if you wish. At 15" (16", 17") you may
decrease about 10 stitches evenly-spaced across the
back only. Purl 1 round to turn hem, and work
2-3" in thinner wool, and on fewer stitches if you
like. Sew down gently, without casting off. Sew
sleeve seams.

FIGURE 110 - GAFFER'S GANSEY GRAPH

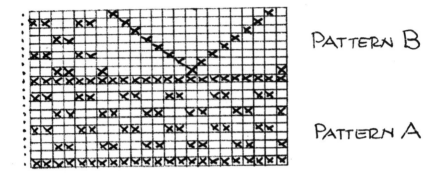

PATTERN B

PATTERN A

Pattern A is knitted once as a border.

Pattern B is repeated vertically to wanted shoulder height.

GAFFER'S FISHERMAN GANSEY

GAUGE: 5 stitches to 1". Get it right.
SIZE: 45" around, 25" long.
MATERIALS: 6 4oz skeins of 2-ply Sheepswool, or
Fisherman wool, or 2-ply "Homespun". A 16" and
24" circular needle to give you the above GAUGE.

CAST ON with 24" needle, 225 stitches, and work
30 rounds of K 2, P 2, (functional, and good for
the character). You may want to use a smaller
size needle for the ribbing.
BEGIN stocking stitch body, and keep side "seams"
an extention of the ribbing by having P 2, K 2, P 2
continue up the sides. This tends to dimple in,
but will block out. Put in several SHORT ROWS
(see page 38) across the back.
AT 14" begin the pattern AND the GUSSETS.
For the latter, increase 1 stitch in the purled
section every 4th round until there are a total
of 20 stitches; put them on a piece of wool.
In their place, CAST ON 2 stitches to take care
of future armhole cutting. From now on keep
6 stitches in stocking-stitch on either side to
provide a smooth vertical edge for the chest-
pattern, as well as a neat area for knitting up
the sleeve stitches.
AT 1" SHY OF WANTED LENGTH, baste,
machine-stitch, and cut armhole (see pages
61 & 62).
JOIN back to front by a knitted-on garter-
stitch strip as follows:
AT LEFTHAND FRONT, Cast On 12 stitches by
12 backward loops, and work back & forth as follows:
K 11, *SSK. Turn. Wool forward, slip 1 stitch as if to
purl, K 10, Wool forward, slip next 2 stitches as if to
Purl. Turn. K 2 together. K 10. Repeat from *.

This makes a neat Garter-Stitch shoulder-strip,
and joins back to front without a seam.
1/3 of it forms the left shoulder, 1/3 the neck,
and 1/3 the right shoulder.
TO RAISE BACK-OF-NECK, increase 1 stitch
by Make 1 at the <u>back</u> every 4th ridge.
LEAVE 6 stitches for the front and work the
neckback straight. PICK UP neck-front-stitches
and work straight to correspond to back.
JOIN AGAIN and work right shoulder, <u>decreasing</u>
every 4th ridge at back.
DO NOT CAST OFF, but immediately knit up
stitches down front of right armhole at the
rate of 2 stitches for every 3 rows; KNIT UP
gusset stitches, and 2 stitches for 3 rows up
armhole back. You should have about 120
stitches.
WORK AROUND on a 16" needle, keeping the
shoulder strip in garter-stitch by purling every
second round and slipping the first and last
stitches purlwise on these rounds.
DECREASE the purled stitches of the gusset
2 every 4th round until they are down to 2;
preserve them for the seamline, and work the
decreases every 4th round in the stocking-
stitch fabric.
AFTER 4" of the upper sleeve, work border
pattern A, and continue in stocking-stitch.
WHEN sleeves are long enough (around 18" for
an adult), they will be the right width for the
wrists.
FINISH them with 30 rounds of K 2, P 2 rib
and CAST OFF in K 2, P 2.
NEATEN the cut edges of the armholes
inside with herringbone or blanket stitch.
FOR SECOND SLEEVE, knit up from the wrong
side of the shoulder-strip, which is practically
undetectible. To be truthful, I hate
knitting sleeves downward from the body, but in
this case, with the charming gussets, and the
continuation of the shoulder-strip, I think it's
worth it.

notes on cardigan boarders — pg. 72

FIGURE 111
NOTE ON PATTERN GRAPH:
Start at the bottom;
work from Right to
Left. Repeat from
double line.
Keep first stitch of
each round in strict
vertical line.

CARRY WOOL LOOSELY.

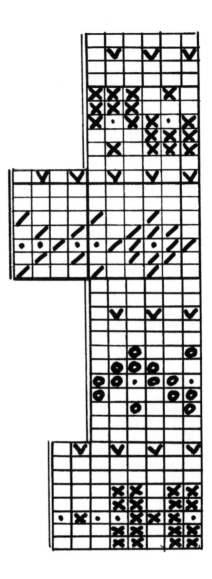

☐ BACKGROUND
☒ MOORIT
⊡ WHITE
▽ LOVAT
⊙ LOCH MAREE
⧄ TARTAN BLUE

V-NECK FAIR ISLE PULLOVER VEST

GAUGE: 6 stitches to 1". Get it right.

MEASUREMENTS: 38" (40", 42") around.
23" (25", 27") long.

MATERIALS: Shetland wool; 5 (6, 7) ounces of main color, 1 ounce each brown, green, blue, lovat and white. You may use 2 shades each in brown, blue and green as on the model.
1 16" and 1 24" circular needle of a size to give you the above GAUGE of 6 sts to 1".

CAST ON with your 24" circular needle 208 (216, 224) stitches. Join, being careful not to twist. K 2, P 2 around for 24 (26, 28) rounds. Increase 20 (24, 28) stitches evenly-spaced around. You now have 228 (240, 252) stitches. Continue in pattern following the graph on the opposite page.

NOTE: In the first blue pattern, work the first and fifth rounds in dark blue; next blue pattern work the first and fifth rounds in the light shade. Alternate shades in all patterns this way for a true Fair Isle sweater.

ARMHOLES: at 12" (14", 16") place 20 (21, 22) stitches on threads at each side. Cast on 4 stitches at this spot and continue around. (This makes a "kangaroo pouch"; see pages 70 & 71.) Decrease 1 stitch each side of the 4 stitches every 2nd round 10 (11, 12) times. NOW:

NECK-SHAPING: Put 3 stitches on a thread at center-front; cast on 4 stitches and work decreases as for armholes (another Kangaroo Pouch). Continue around to 23" (25", 27") or wanted length, stopping at the end of a pattern with a plain round. Put all stitches on a thread.

BASTE down center of the 4 stitches at armholes and neck. MACHINE-STITCH two rows of small stitches each side of basting. CUT armholes and neck on basting.

WEAVE shoulders. With 16" needle knit up stitches around armholes at the rate of 2 stitches for every 3 rounds. Work 10 rounds in K 2, P 2 rib, and cast off loosley.

WORK NECK in the same way, but on the first round, work to within 1 stitch of center-stitch, Slip 2 together knitwise, K 1, P2SSO (see page 30). Repeat this decrease every second round, keeping the stitches on either side in ribbing.

PRESS cut edges toward body and neaten with cross-stitch.

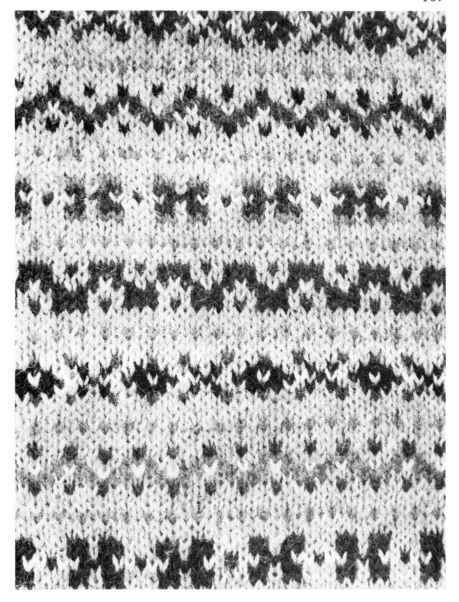

FIGURE 112
Close-up of the patterns used in STU'S FAIR ISLE.

GLOSSARY

AMERICAN-STYLE KNITTING : The wool is held in the right hand or over the right forefinger, wound around the righthand-needle from back to front, and fished through each stitch on the lefthand needle.

ARAN KNITTING: The traditional knitting textures of the fisherman off the Western Irish coast. Unbleached cream-colored wool was used, and the jerseys were wrought in the most elaborate and significant variations of cables.

BACK OF NECK SHAPING: About the most vital spot in any sweater; short rows are worked across the neck back -- two stitches longer every row, back and forth, until at least 3/4" has been added.

BOHUS KNITTING: Imaginative and wonderful patterns in a Swedish craft from the middle of the 20th century. Some overall patterns were strict and geometric, and some sweaters had yokes and matching caps of an indescribable beauty employing many subtly harmonizing colors, regularly-spaced purled stitches, and slipped stitches. These are practically unreproduceable. The finest wools were used at a very small gauge. Emma Jacobson was the founder and leading spirit of this contemporary folk-art. If you own one of these pieces you have an heirloom and a treasure.

BUTTONHOLE - 1-ROW: See page 73.

BUTTONHOLE - 3-ROW: (worked back and forth). Row 1: cast off 3 stitches. Row 2: Cast on 3 stitches by 3 backward loops. Pick up first cast-off stitch, place it on lefthand needle. Knit 2 together. Row 3: Knit into the back of the 3 cast-on loops and also into the stitch following them.

CASTING-ON CASTING-OFF: A way of duplicating casting-on by casting-off. (see page 50)

CASTING-ON, LONGTAIL: The best and the best-known

method; fish the long tail through a series of backward loops formed on the righthand needle.

CAST OFF: To finish off stitches so that they will not run: Knit 2 stitches * with tip of lefthand needle pull 1st stitch over 2nd stitch. Knit 1, repeat from *. (To make neat corner ending work the last two stitches together.) N.B. Ribbing should be cast off by working the K and P stitches as they present themselves. For a fine smooth cast-off, see Casting-on Casting-off, page 50.

CAST ON: To place the very first row of stitches on the needle.

CONTINENTAL KNITTING: The wool is held over the left forefinger, and hooked through each stitch with the righthand needle.

DARN IN ENDS: With a very large sharp needle skim all ends for 1-2" diagonally through the back surface of the knitted fabric. Snip off. For perfection, split each wool-end into its component plies for this purpose, and darn them in like a spider.

DECREASE (DECR): Knit 2 together, OR SSK: slip 2 stitches separately knitwise, put the tip of the lefthand needle into them from left to right, and knit them together from this position. This last is a vastly improved version of "K 2 together through the back loops" which is primitive, not to say erroneous.

DOUBLE DECREASE (DBL DECR): Slip 1, Knit 2 together, pass slipped stitch over. OR: Slip 2 together, Knit 1, Pass 2 slipped stitches over. OR: K 3 together.

DOUBLE INCREASE (DBL INC): At side "seams". You may like to leave 5 stitches between the two increases instead of 3. Three makes them a little bit close to the subsequent phoney seam, and a slight occasinal error of one stitch could entangle the phoney seam with the increase. see page 16.

FAIR ISLE KNITTING: From the Northern Scottish Islands, in muted colors of browns, greens and cream. The

colors vary within each pattern, and also, most idio-
syncratically, within the background at the same
time. The wool is rarely carried for more than 5
stitches. Brighter colors are now being introduced.
Which is a pity. See Sarah Don and Tristan.

FAROE KNITTING: Related to Norwegian knitting, but usually with extremely simple patterns and short carrying of the wool. Most frequently in the natural
sheep colors of cream, brown, beige and blacksheep.
Shoulders are dropped and sleevetops straight. See
FØROYSK BINDINGARMYNSTER.

FISHERMEN'S JERSEYS, GUERNSEYS AND/OR GANSEYS:
Dark blue or black sweaters with the shoulders and
upper sleeves heavily embossed with knit-and-purl
patterns and occasional cables. They were worn by
fishermen all around the coast of the British Isles.
The name(s) are derived from those of the Channel
Islands, where there once flourished a large handknitting industry.

GAUGE: The number of stitches or fractions of a stitch to
1 inch measured horizontally. Row gauge is less
significent, and is governed by the stitch-gauge anyway. Gauge may vary depending on the size of
needle used, the thickness of the wool, and the ten-
sion of the individual knitter. In directions recom-
mending a certain wool at a certain gauge, vary the
needle-size until you achieve it. If you are choosing
your own gauge and your own garment-size, you may
be much more flexible.

GRAPH PAPER, KNITTER'S: This is governed by the proportions of an individual knitted stitch, which is
wider that it is high, so that the graphed spaces
are oblong instead of square. Invaluable for graphing
designs that will not distort into flattened widened
versions when knitted.

ICELANDIC KNITTING typically uses natural-colored, totally
unspun wool from the Icelandic Sheep, which have a
very long fleece (some staples are up to 8" long -
the WARMEST wool I've ever met.) The hallmark of
Icelandic sweaters is a deep, elaborately-patterned yoke

and seamless construction except for a short underarm seam, which we weave to make it totally seamless.

I-CORD: A very narrow tube of stocking-stitch, formed by working these stitches over and over from right to left, and pulling the wool firmly across the back after each unturned row. It is usually made on 3 stitches, but may be worked on 4, 5, or even 6 stitches. With more stitches, a kind of ladder or runner is formed up the back, which can, however, be hooked up later with a crochet hook. (I did make a pair of gloves with I-Cord fingers on 9 stitches, but shall not do this again.)

INCREASE (INC): Make 1 (M1): put a backward loop, or half-hitch over the righthand needle. When these increases are paired, they may be twisted in opposing directions. A related increase to the foregoing: Pick up the running thread between the stitches and knit into the back of it. This is tantamount to having worked a M1 in the previous row. OR: Put the wool over the righthand needle from front to back. This loop is knitted into on the following row and forms a hole, as in lace knitting - or a baby's buttonhole. OR: Knit into the front and back of the stitch, which forms a bar next to the stitch and is not generally advisable.

KNIT (K): To pull the working wool through the stitch on the lefthand needle from the back to the front, forming a smooth new stitch on the righthand needle.

KNITSCH: An irregularity or a knitting-glitsch (thank you Jean Krebs).

KNIT UP: Along a selvedge or other edge, fish through a series of loops onto the righthand needle where they will form stitches. For the correct relationship when picking up and knitting a vertical garter-stitch border on a horizontal stocking-stitch body, pick up 2 stitches for every 3 rows.

NEEDLE-GAUGE: A piece of metal or plastic with holes calibrated to the various needle-sizes: U.S. #0000 to #16. European $1\frac{1}{4}$mm to 9mm.

NEEDLES, KNITTING: In pairs with knobs for working back-and-forth; in sets of 4 pointed at both ends for knitting around on socks or mittens (sets of 5 in Europe); circular with firm ends and flexible center-sections for circular or back-and-forth knitting, in short, for everything but socks and mittens. 16" long for caps, baby-sweaters and sleeves, 24" long for everything else.

NEEDLES, SEWING: Should be quite large for using with knitted fabric. Blunt points are useful for weaving (grafting) and for most kinds of sewing-up. Sharp points are necessary for darning in ends.

NORWEGIAN KNITTING: The art of knitting patterns with two colors alternately in regular repeats with fairly strong colors. Traditionally only two colors are employed at once, and the wool is extremely rarely carried for more than five stitches. These two rules may be broken, but only for very good cause. The sweaters have dropped-shoulders and cut armholes. See NORWEGIAN KNITTING DESIGNS.

PASS SLIPPED STITCH OVER (PSSO): Slip 1 stitch, Knit 1 stitch, Pass the Slipped Stitch Over the knit stitch.

PLY: The number of threads which are twisted to form the wool.

PHONEY SEAMS: A raised vertical row of stitches used to demark and indicate where seamlines would be if the garment were not circular. The seam-stitch may be slipped every third round, or, better, dropped before being cast-off or joined, and hooked up again with a crochet hook, alternately two stitches and one stitch.

PICK UP: Along a selvedge or other edge, pick up stitches by putting the righthand needle through them. Frequently mistaken for "knit up".

PURL: To pull the working wool through the stitch on the lefthand needle from the front to the back forming a bumpy new stitch on the righthand needle.

ROW FINDER, MAGNETIC: A sanity-saving device. Its page-sized metal sheet is placed under your knitting directions and held in place by a long narrow magnet, which is moved down, line by line, as your knitting progresses, to show you where you are.

SEW UP: To join two pieces of knitting, optimally performed from the right side: with a blunt sewing needle take up alternate stitches or loops from two selvedges or borders You may also put the blunt needle down through one stitch and up through the next and repeat this on alternate sides. For the next stitch, put the needle down through the stitch up through which you came the time before, and up through the next stitch. Rather like weaving or Kitchener Stitch.

SHORT ROWS: are inserted in knitted fabric, usually by twos. They are mostly used for lengthening the back of a sweater, and are worked in pairs every few inches.

SLIP (SL): To transfer a stitch from the lefthand needle to the righthand needle without working it.

SSK: (see DECREASE)

SSKK: SLIP, SLIP, KNIT, KREBS: Jean Krebs' most recent unvention. It has not been consumer-tested for long, but it would be a shame to withhold it. It is used to make a left-leaning decrease even smoother than does SSK: Slip 2 stitches knitwise, put the tip of the left-hand needle into them from the front , and knit them together from this position. Slightly slower, but appreciably amoother. Thanks, Jean.

STITCH (ST): The loops of wool on the needle.

TOGETHER (TOG): Knit the stitches together through the fronts of the loops unless otherwise specified.

UNBLEACHED: The natural wool as it comes from the sheep, scoured but not bleached or dyed, usually cream-colored, but sometimes a shade of brown. (Any color darker than cream is known as Blacksheep by shepherds.)

UNSPUN: Wool which has not been spun or twisted. It pulls apart quite easily, but once knitted is strong.

WEAVING, or GRAFTING, or KITCHENER-STITCH: The joining of two pieces of un-cast-off knitting by inserting an extra "row" with a blunt needle threaded with wool. In stocking-stitch or garter-stitch any two edges may be woven, but in pattern-stitches of any kind two tops or bottoms can NOT be joined perfectly.

WEAVING, 1st STITCH OF: Once you have mastered weaving, consult MARY THOMAS p. 171. on dealing with the first stitch of this technique: Start by coming UP through the first stitch of the lower piece, and then DOWN through the first stitch of the upper piece. Then continue as described in WEAVING, above and on p. 49.

WOOLEN: Yarn made from fibers which run in several directions; more fluffy than worsted.

WORSTED: Yarn made from fibers which have been combed to run smoothly parallel to each other.

WRAPPING: A trick employed to eliminate the holes caused by turning at the end of each short row. See p. 38.

INDEX

All the wools and books
used in the
KNITTING WORKSHOP
were supplied by
MEG SWANSEN.